Abolish Money (From Economics)!

Brian Romanchuk

Published by BondEconomics, Canada
www.BondEconomics.com

Published by BondEconomics, 2017, Montréal, Québec.

Library and Archives Canada
Abolish Money (From Economics)!
Brian Romanchuk 1968-
ISBN: 978-0-9947480-7-2 Epub Edition
ISBN: 978-0-9947480-6-5 Kindle Edition
ISBN: 978-0-9947480-8-9 Paperback Edition

Contents

List of Figures

Acknowledgements

I would like to thank the readers of my articles at BondEconomics.com for their feedback. Portions of this text previously appeared as articles on that site, and I have been able to incorporate suggestions and corrections.I would also like to thank Judy Yelon for her editing of this text.

Finally, any errors and omissions are my own.

Part I Money and Its Discontents

1 Introduction

This book is not a proposal for real-world economic reform; rather, it is a plea to reform the theoretical basis of macroeconomics. In particular, the argument is that we need to jettison the concept of money from economic theory, and turn our focus on what really matters in modern industrial capitalist economies. My objective is to demonstrate how economic discussion has been warped by a focus on money.

I am not particularly optimistic about my reform goals; academic economics is remarkably resistant to common sense. However, if they were realised, the improvements to theory might lead to improvements in the real world. Policymakers have wasted decades pursuing pointless gradations to monetary policy because of bad theory; it may be that we might once again have sensible economic policies if we have sensible economic theories to base them on.

Anyone who has read a great deal of economic commentary knows that there are many crackpot theories floating around on the internet and in financial newsletters. Although I am highly skeptical about mainstream macroeconomics, I am normally on their side when compared to the crackpots. However, once the subject of money comes up, mainstream economists are the major producers of dubious theories. Unfortunately, these theories end up being entertained by central bankers, and we end up with economic policies that can only be understood as a form of ceremonial magic.

To remove magic from economics, we need to drop the mysticism around money. Yes, we live in a monetary economy. That said, industrial capitalism relies upon well-defined property rights enshrined in law; but we do not attempt to shoehorn the Supreme Court into our models. If money is going to show up within the models, it has to have useful properties for explaining economic outcomes. However, money data are not particularly informative, and so the concept needs to be de-emphasised.

About this book

The format of this book is experimental; it consists of articles that were either published in draft form on BondEconomics.com (one section is based on an appendix of another book), or are appearing for the first time. I consider 10 out of the other 22 articles to be new material (although many of the remaining articles were heavily revised). Since the sections are meant to be self-contained and not necessarily read in order, there is a certain amount of repetition of some themes.

Some time series charts appear in roughly the same form in different sections of the book. This repetition is needed because standard e-readers currently do not support a "go-back" operation. As a result, there is no convenient way to refer to a figure that appears some distance from the referring text.

Although I am pleased (and somewhat surprised) to have academic readers, I have dispensed with an academic tradition – the bibliography. I have instead put the bibliographic information in the most convenient place – endnotes for the e-book edition and footnotes in the paperback edition. For most e-book readers, you lose your current reading position if you jump to a bibliography. This decision means that the same reference information can appear more than once. This repetition should only be noticeable to readers who browse the endnotes in order.

Finally, please note that I use Canadian spelling and grammatical conventions, which are a mixture of English and American custom.

Montréal, Québec, Canada, December 8, 2016.

2 Abolish Money [From Economics]!

This essay was not previously published.

We live in a monetary economy. For good or for ill, we judge economic outcomes in terms of money, and most citizens spend a significant portion of their time "making money." It is not surprising that "money" plays an important role within economics.

My argument is that this role has become too important, and has warped economists' ability to think about the economy. The important psychological role of "money" within society has been transferred to monetary aggregates, and they are given far more significance than they deserve. We need to become indifferent to money within economic models – "amonetarist."

Take any question of economic reform that has recently been endorsed by economists in or near the mainstream, and the odds are that "money" is involved. Mainstream economists have wasted an incredible amount of time discussing Quantitative Easing, Positive Money, and Helicopter Money, instead of discussing policies that might have had a chance to deal with the actual problems facing society. If we go back a few decades, incredible damage was done because of the daft belief that central banks could control the "money supply." Meanwhile, there is incredible anger about the nature of "money" at the political fringes; either people are mad that banks create "money," or by the fact that "money" is something other than a precious metal.

As a post-Keynesian, I would note that mainstream economists have been the worst offenders of proposing magical monetary solutions to real-world problems. This is ironic, as one of the alleged theoretical insights of mainstream economics was that money is a neutral veil over what really mattered: the production and distribution of real goods and services. This is presumably a side effect of the earlier infatuation with Monetarism.

The Solution: Abolish Money

The best way forward for economics is to abolish money as a concept from macroeconomics. We presumably would need to keep the concept of the unit of account, but that is just an accounting convention. Instead of discussing "money," we would be left with various instruments, which may or may not be components of various monetary aggregates. In Part IV of this book, I discuss how this would be accomplished in more detail.

With money gone as a concept, we are forced to roll up our sleeves and analyse how those real-world financial instruments behave, and not just project our fantasies upon them. We would then be able to analyse the effects of policies upon the economy, rather than debating jibber-jabber like "the central bank will permanently increase the monetary base."

As an added bonus, the phrase "monetary policy" would be thrown into the dustbin, along with all the various vacuous debates as to which actions qualify as representing "monetary policy." We would have to discuss what the central bank actually does, which, in modern developed economies, is "interest rate policy."

The advantages of moving away from money are discussed at greater length in the other essays within this volume. Key examples include the following points.

- Once we get rid of money, we largely get rid of the decades-old arcane debate whether it is "exogenous" or "endogenous." We need to look at whether the central bank can control the amount outstanding of various instruments.
- If money no longer exists as a concept, we no longer worry whether it is "neutral" or not.
- We no longer care what instruments are included in the "money supply," a question that has vexed anyone who has tried to relate economic theory to the real world.
- The Quantity Theory of Money will no longer be there to fool the gullible.
- We will no longer face silly questions about what money really is, such as being a zero-coupon perpetual, or whether it is or not debt.
- We will stop attaching mystical abilities to bank reserves.
- We will no longer care whether gold is money; we will instead ask ourselves whether a price control system for gold makes sense. (Spoiler: no.)
- We have no reason to care about banks' privileged ability to

"create money"; we will instead look at the best way of regulating the entire financial system.

- Monetarists would have avoided the embarrassment of "money supply targeting."
- There would have been no reason to expect Quantitative Easing to accomplish anything different than changing the maturity profile of government debt. Such maturity shifts happen all of the time, and have had no measurable effect on anything.
- "Helicopter Money" would not exist, and proponents of the policy would have to explain how a central bank with absolutely no expertise in distribution programmes is going to hand out cheques to the populace in an efficient fashion.
- The proponents of "Positive Money" would need to stop complaining about banks' privileged ability to create money, and explain what real-world problem would be solved by requiring 100% government collateral backing one type of financial liability issued by one type of financial institution.
- Economists who are concerned about developments in the twenty-first century will stop arguing about the modes of Babylonian commerce.

How Can This Be Done?

Implementation of this reform is straightforward: we go through economic models and arguments, and eliminate the use of the term "money." Where it appears, we replace it with something that is more directly related to the real world.

For example, we can have models where the private sector holds a certain percentage of its portfolio in currency (that is, notes and coins, which pay no interest). Since such holdings are suboptimal when interest rates are positive, there will need to be some factor that favours currency holdings within the behavioural equations. Since we would also need similar factors that drive the split between bonds and bills (and equities versus fixed income), I would not view this as being "special treatment." For example, we need to consider such holdings if we want to simulate the effects of seigneurage in fiscal projections. In any event, these model concepts are directly mapped to the behaviour of real-world instruments, and not to a poorly defined "money supply."

One argument against the abolition of money is that we need "money" as a means of exchange within the economy. Although this is probably true, this confuses the real-world and economic models. Macroeconomic models cannot hope to model the intricacies of the underlying transactions of an economy, or the details of the payments system. (Of course, one could build a model of the payments system, but it would be implausible that such a detailed model can tell us anything about macroeconomic behaviour.) In a tractable economic model, all transactions within an accounting period are going to clear simultaneously; that is, we do not track every transaction. Since all transactions settle simultaneously, there is no need for any particular monetary instrument to allow transactions.[1] As noted in the introduction, industrial capitalism needs a legal system to function, yet we do not try to insert a court system into economic models.

Some might insist that we need to model "money" as being special, as it makes transactions easier. For example, we might want to demonstrate how money improves the welfare of shipwreck survivors on a tropical island who might otherwise insist on the use of barter. (I would argue that such a reversion to barter is unlikely, but I will put that objection to the side for now.) Although it might be true that money leads to more efficient outcomes than barter – who cares? The concerns of people stranded on an island have no practical relevance for the analysis of modern capitalist economies.

The abolition of money from economic theory is less radical than it appears. Within the analysis produced by "market economists," money numbers are now largely ignored. To a certain extent, this reform would bring academic and internet economics in line with "best practices" in the financial industry.

Collateral Damage

As always, there are trade-offs involved. Some useful bits of economics might be lost amidst the sea of inanities that would be abolished. However, my feeling is that the losses would be marginal.

I am in the Modern Monetary Theory (MMT) theoretical camp, and so I am most familiar with that body of thought. The most obvious

---

1   Since all transactions between all sectors are assumed to occur simultaneously, there is no problem associated with the "double coincidence of wants."

loss for MMT is that it would have to come up with a new moniker, as "monetary" is abolished along with "money." My guess is that it could be replaced with "Modern Currency Theory" without much of a loss.

- Much of MMT's analysis revolves around the *currency* regime, in that it discusses the advantages of free-floating exchange rates.
- There is a great deal of detailed MMT analysis of the operational realities behind government liability management. Those details survive the purge of generic "money."
- MMT is closely associated with the school of thought known as "Chartalism" or "neo-Chartalism" – which is the "state theory of money." As I argue in "Should We Care About the Origins of Money?" the important part of Chartalism is answering the question of why people offer real goods and services in exchange for government liabilities that cannot be redeemed for anything other than government liabilities. This question survives the disappearance of "money."

Other schools of thought will also have to adapt. For example, take Marx's famous M-C-M' description of capitalism – capitalists trade money for commodities (capital) in order to make more money. We can rephrase this to the more straightforward formula: in capitalism, capitalists try to make a profit (which is defined in terms of income flows). Although that might seem to be obvious to anyone operating in the real world, it is actually an insight when compared to the view that profits are always and everywhere zero (as the result of dubious theoretical reasons).

Monetarism (to the extent it still exists) would be hardest hit by this reform. However, as I argue in "Would Eliminating Money From Monetarism Have Stopped It From Jumping the Shark?," such a change would have been for the better. The school of thought would have needed a new name, but it would have fit into mainstream economics without the various embarrassments of the 1980s.

"Amonetarism," not Anti-Monetarism

I initially wanted to describe my views as being "anti-Monetarist," as I was opposed to the Monetarist elevation of the importance of money in economics. However, I realised that my view is not that money is extremely unimportant, rather that it may or may not be important, depending on the context.

The best way forward is to be indifferent towards money, which implies that we need to be "amonetarist."

Part II Primers

3 Banks and Money

This essay has not been previously published.

It is safe to say that the relationship between private banks and money causes a great deal of confusion. In this essay, I discuss some of the ideas that I find cause the most difficulty. More advanced related topics are discussed in later sections.

Bank Deposits are Money

One of the difficulties with money as a concept within economics is that its meaning is vague. The closest we have to a precise definition are the monetary aggregates (M1, M2, etc.). (I discuss these aggregates in the following essay.) Bank deposits are included in all but the narrowest monetary aggregates, and so we can consider them to be money.

Other financial instruments are also included in wider monetary aggregates. However, bank deposits have legal advantages versus those other instruments. For example, the expectation is that debts will be repaid via a deposit transfer of some sort (cheque, electronic transfer). However, a great many transactions can be intermediated without the use of bank deposits, and so we cannot argue that they have some unique properties.

Bank Lending Creates Deposits

Bank lending is the usual means by which the aggregate amount of bank deposits outstanding increases. (The alternatives are that government-issued currency – notes and coins – are deposited, or that a government-issued cheque is cashed.)

When you take out a bank loan of $100, the bank will grow both its assets and liabilities by $100 – it increases the amount you have deposited by $100 (which is a $100 increase in the bank liabilities), and it adds a bank loan (payable by you) to its assets.[2] (If the previous summary is

---

2   There are variations. If you have a line of credit, you would only create the deposit when you draw on the credit line; until this point, the credit line is an off balance sheet item. If you have an overdraft, you create

too brief, the mechanism by which bank lending creates loans is discussed in greater depth in "No, Banks Do Not Lend Reserves" – Section 13.)

In most cases, that increase in your deposit balance is temporary – you generally want to take out a loan to purchase something, not to increase your bank deposit balance. If you use your increased cash balance to purchase something, the deposit is transferred to the seller's account. Such a transfer leaves total bank deposits unchanged, so that the aggregate amount of deposits is higher than it was before the loan was made.

Repaying a bank loan reverses the process; the amount deposited decreases while cancelling out the bank loan. Under the normal circumstances of growing nominal incomes, more loans are granted than are paid back within an accounting period, causing aggregate deposit growth.

Since the act of granting a loan does not require the use of real resources, there is no fundamental economic constraint upon the creation of bank deposit money. This is in contrast to commodity money (such as gold coins), where the commodity needs to be extracted and processed in order to allow it to be manufactured into monetary instruments. Instead, the constraints on bank deposit creation are financial.

If there were only a single bank, there would be almost no financial constraints on money creation. However, in real-world economies, the reality is that when a bank grants a loan, it has to expect that the deposit money created will be transferred to another bank. This is discussed further in "No, Banks Do Not Lend Reserves."

Bank Reserves

Bank reserves are commonly referred to in economics discussions; they are deposits held by private banks at the central bank. *(Please note that bank reserves have no relationship to loan loss reserves held by banks.)* Since not all countries have reserve requirements, "bank reserves" may not be the best term; the more general phrasing is "settlement balances at the central bank." However, since the United States still has reserve requirements, you are more likely to run across the expression "reserves" rather than "settlement balances."

Bank reserves typically do not pay any interest, which makes them an unattractive asset. The usual reason why banks hold them is that they are required

---

a negative deposit value, which is balanced by the increase in the deposit balance of whomever you sent the payment to.

to do so; the level of required reserves is equal to some fraction of certain classes of deposits held at the bank. (In a financial crisis, banks would rather leave deposits at the central bank than lend to other private sector firms.)

Since required reserves are a fixed fraction of deposits (or certain classes of deposits), older economic textbooks flipped the relationship to argue that deposits are a fixed multiple of deposits at the central bank. This was known as the *money multiplier*. For example, if required reserves are 10% of deposits, we then will see aggregate deposits are 10 times the amount of required reserves in the banking system. Since it appears that the central bank has some control over the amount of reserves within the financial system, some economists inferred that the central bank can control the amount of bank deposits outstanding.

This belief is discussed in later essays; my summary is that the belief is incorrect. Moreover, bank reserves have been abolished in countries like Canada, without any ill effects. A 0% reserve requirement implies an infinite money multiplier, which blows up the old textbook models.

Operationally, reserves are just a form of a tax on the formal banking system; banks are forced to lend to the central bank at a below market rate of interest. As I discuss in "Positive Money" (Section 15), required reserves do not ensure that a bank has a strong liquidity position; the bank has to have an excess amount of liquid assets beyond the regulatory minimum in order to be liquid. The only way that required reserves help banking system liquidity is that if the reserve ratios are lowered in a crisis, the freed up reserves act as a new buffer of excess liquidity for banks. This is just a form of regulatory forbearance.[3]

In recent years, some central banks have made large purchases of assets, which results in their balance sheets growing (as discussed in "Primer: Quantitative Easing" – Section 6). This shows up as an excess of deposits at the central bank over what is required by bank reserve regulations – *excess reserves*.

What Limits Deposit Growth?

There are two internal factors that constrain the growth of bank balance sheets (and hence deposit growth).

- Bank capital requirements; and

---

3   "Regulatory forbearance" is the polite way of saying "bending the rules to bail out incompetent bankers."

- the liquidity management needs of banks, taking into account *all* liquid instruments (bank reserves being only one such instrument).

Please note that neither of them depends upon banks holding "money" in order to grant loans, which does not match the standard intuition about lending.

However, in the current economic environment, the true constraint upon loan growth is an external factor – the willingness of creditworthy customers to borrow. (It is always possible to find non-creditworthy entities that want to borrow money.) This willingness to increase debt is typically the result of increasing fixed investment. The implication is that deposit growth reflects the strength of the economic cycle, and is not a *cause* of growth (the cause is the increased willingness to invest).

The reason why willingness to borrow is currently the constraint, rather than liquidity or bank capital, is that the modern financial system is swamped by investors looking for a place to allocate their financial asset holdings. They are desperate to hit their return targets, as current demographics create a large demand for retirement income. If banks were short of capital in order to meet regulatory requirements, it would be easy for them to raise it in public markets. Equity in a well-run bank is an ideal investment for yield-starved investors.

Liquidity constraints (such as bank reserves or broader liquid asset ratio regulations) are also largely non-binding. Liquid assets do not require much capital to be held against them, while the only cost is that they have a lower running yield than a loan book. The need to hold liquid assets is a cost of doing business for banks, and this cost is incorporated into bank lending spreads. Very simply, no one worries about the liquidity position of a bank – unless it is about to go bankrupt, in which case it is too late to build up a liquidity buffer.

Concluding Remarks

Since the amount of currency issued by modern governments is small, the bulk of "money" in an economy consists of bank deposits. Banks have some special privileges related to the "moneyness" of their deposit liabilities, but they face stricter regulations than the rest of the financial system.

4 Primer: Monetary Aggregates

This appeared on BondEconomics.com on November 30, 2016.

Mysticism about money is damaging to economic theory. This shows up in even the most fundamental questions, such as defining what "money" really is. It is clear that the developed countries are "monetary societies," and behaviour is very different from those societies where money is either not used or highly ceremonial in nature. Unfortunately, our usage of the word money is often muddled, as we say things like "she made a lot of money selling used cars," even though what we really mean is that "she earned a high income selling used cars." For those with an interest in describing macroeconomic behaviour, such vagueness is not enough; we have to pin down what we mean by money.

If money were to be abolished from economic theory, the only remaining references to money would be the discussion of monetary aggregates. This primer explains the definitions of these aggregates (without diving into the institutional differences between different regions).

Monetary Aggregates

Different jurisdictions have slightly different definitions of monetary aggregates, reflecting different institutional and accounting norms. The aggregate definitions start with an aggregate with the narrowest list of instruments, and then later definitions add more instruments. These are usually labelled M0, M1, M2, M3, with M0 being the narrowest definition. It is also referred to as the "monetary base" (or "base money").

The European Central Bank uses the following broad definitions for M1 - M3 (Figure 1 on page 18).[4]

- M1: currency in circulation (notes and coins), and overnight deposits.
- M2: instruments in M1, plus deposits with an agreed maturity up to 2 years, and deposits redeemable at a period of notice up

4   URL for European Central Bank page listing monetary aggregate definitions: https://www.ecb.europa.eu/stats/money/aggregates/aggr/html/hist.en.html

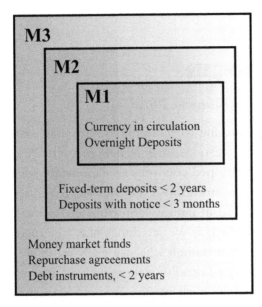

Figure 1. *Monetary Aggregates.*

to 3 months.

- M3: instruments in M2, plus repurchase agreements ("repos"), money market funds, and debt instruments up to 2-year maturity.

The definition of the *monetary base* (M0) is not given by the ECB in the above reference, but for Canadian data, the definition is "notes and coin in circulation, chartered bank and other Canadian Payments Association members' deposits with the Bank of Canada."[5]

The Canadian definition of the monetary base is similar to that for the United States, but there is a key practical difference. In Canada, banks are not required to hold deposits at the central bank (the Bank of Canada), while in the United States, banks are required to hold reserves at the Federal Reserve banks. This means that the definition in the United States would be modified to include "required reserves and excess reserves" (excess reserves being deposits at the central bank in excess of reserve requirements, which are based on the size of bank's deposit base).

Although it may not be obvious, the size of the monetary base is (roughly) equal to the size of the liabilities on the balance sheet of the central bank, since the instruments in the monetary base are liabilities of the central bank.[6] However, not all liabilities of the central bank are included in the monetary base, such as money deposited by the Treasury. That said, we can summarise the situation by saying that operations that expand the central bank's balance sheet generally expand the monetary base (the ex-

---

5   Definition of monetary base from CANSIM table 176-0025.

6   Some people object to viewing the monetary base as being a "liability," but redefining it as anything else makes governmental accounting hard to understand.

ceptions being things like intra-governmental borrowing).

Since a central bank in a floating exchange rate regime generally has control over which transactions it enters into, we can say that the central bank has control over the size of the monetary base. (If the currency is not free-floating, the central bank can be forced to undertake operations to preserve the currency peg. For example, it might be forced to buy/sell gold as part of a gold peg. In which case, the central bank has only partial control over the size of its balance sheet.) The extent of that control is a point of debate within economics (known as "endogenous money" versus "exogenous money" in economist jargon; please see Section 10).

Relating Aggregates to Economic Activity

The only reason to care about monetary aggregates is that we can relate them to other economic variables. By themselves, they are only of interest to accountants ("how many $20 bills did we print, anyway?").

The Quantity Theory of Money in its simplest form argues that we can directly relate the price level in the economy to the money supply. The simplest version of the theory (in which increases in the money supply create proportional increases in the price level) can be rejected by the empirical data, using any of the monetary aggregates to stand in for the vaguely defined "money supply" (as seen in Section 7). However, it is possible to conceive of more complicated relationships between monetary aggregates and the price level, in which increases of money translate into inflation "in the long run."

This search for such statistical relationships explains why there are so many monetary aggregates. Since existing aggregates failed to have predictive powers, new aggregates were developed, which were supposed to cover up the defects of the existing aggregates by adding in new "monetary" instruments. However, these new aggregates also generally failed to be useful as well. As a result, the attractiveness of Monetarism collapsed (although a few rebranded "Market Monetarists" remain), and most analysts pay little attention to the monetary aggregates. The empirical relationships are discussed in "Instability of Money Velocity" and "Should We Care About Money Growth?" (Sections 7 and 8).

Concluding Remarks

Discussions of "money" within macroeconomics are often detached from reality. We need to decide which monetary aggregate to analyse, and then attempt to see whether it provides any useful information about economic behaviour. As I discuss in later sections, we find that the information provided by monetary aggregates is extremely limited, which explains why they are now rarely discussed in market analysis.

5 Primer: Money Neutrality and Velocity

This essay has not been previously published.

Big errors start from smaller ones. In economics, the plausible concepts of money neutrality and the velocity of money have led to many problems. This essay defines these concepts; I discuss the difficulties with them in later sections.

Money Neutrality

The idea of *money neutrality* is simple: monetary values are a unit of measurement for market transactions, and that if we change the units of measurement, it does not affect the real value of transactions.

There is a simple real-world experiment that appears to validate this idea: currency redenomination. For example, General Charles de Gaulle of France created the *nouveau franc* on January 1, 1960, by striking the last two digits off calculations of existing French *francs* in circulation.[7] In other words, a *nouveau franc* is just 100 old *francs*, and contracts were adjusted to compensate. The objective was to return nominal prices back to what feel like "normal" levels after inflation.

It is clear that just multiplying all monetary values by some constant is not going to make people better off – other than the convenience value of returning prices to levels that people consider to be "normal." Within an economic model, the implication is that if we scale monetary values by some constant, the model dynamics for real variables should not be changed. That is, the model output is neutral with respect to the monetary unit.

Formally defining money neutrality is difficult (outside of a currency redenomination). This is discussed further in "The Incoherence of Money Neutrality" (Section 11). For the present, I will stick with a hand-waving definition: changing the stock of money (in a real-world economy, or in an economic model) will not affect real variables. (Although this is close to the definitions normally used, the previously referenced essay explains why

7   Milton Friedman, on page 21 of *Money Mischief: Episodes in Monetary History*. Published by Harcourt Brace Jovanovich, 1992.

this definition is problematic.)

The concept is quite often broken down into *long-run* and *short-run* neutrality. Models such as Real Business Cycle models have the property that changes in money have no effect on real variables at any time, which is the definition of short-run neutrality (money is neutral, even in the short run). However, it is unclear whether Real Business Cycles are anything other than an elaborate practical joke.

Long-run money neutrality is more commonly encountered. The argument is that operations that change the money stock may have a short-term effect on real economic variables, but in the long term, the only effect on changes in monetary aggregates is via changes in the price level.

Velocity of Money

Money velocity is a concept that has caused considerable grief. Although we can always calculate the "velocity of money," it is unclear whether it is useful in practice. If velocity were constant, the classical Quantity Theory of Money would result.

Within the history of monetary economics, the equation

$$M \cdot V = P \cdot Q$$

is of utmost importance. Within the equation, M stands for the money supply, V for the *velocity of money*, P for the price level, and Q for the quantity of output. The quantity $P \cdot Q$ is the dollar value of output (price times quantity), or nominal GDP. The intuition is that the velocity is the number of times the money supply circulates in a year.

If velocity were constant, we could use this equation to develop strong conclusions about the relationship between the money supply and nominal GDP (and the price level). Doubling the money supply would double nominal GDP.

Furthermore, if we accept that money neutrality is at least roughly correct, we would expect real output (Q) to be largely unaffected by the doubling of the money supply. In which case, the implication of a constant velocity is that the price level (P) would (at least roughly) double. This matches the simpler definitions of the *Quantity Theory of Money*.

Of course, if we note the difficulties associated with exogenous money previously noted, the value of this insight is limited – how exactly is the money supply going to double?

In any event, empirical analysis shows us that velocity is nowhere near constant. This empirical analysis is pursued at greater length in "Instability of Money Velocity."

Concluding Remarks

Money neutrality and the velocity of money appear to be reasonable concepts. The difficulty is attempting to apply them to the real world.

6 Primer: Quantitative Easing

This section is a modified version of text that previously appeared as Section 5.4 of Understanding Government Finance; the section on Qualitative Easing was added.

Quantitative Easing (QE) is a rather silly central bank practice that became popular after the Financial Crisis. It had previously been adopted by the Bank of Japan during its battle with deflation, but then it was undertaken by the United States Federal Reserve, which was desperate to remain relevant after it had lowered its policy rate to zero. The importance of Quantitative Easing to the economy rests almost solely upon how it affects the beliefs of financial market participants about the future.

From the perspective of an anthropologist, this could only be described as a form of magic. This magic only works if investors impute mysterious properties to the monetary base. Abolishing "money" from economic theory would have the result of forcing investors to understand what is really happening (not a whole lot).

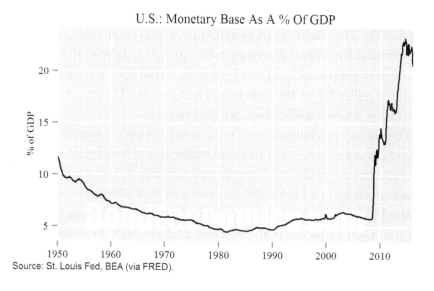

Figure 2. *U.S. Monetary base after Quantitative Easing.*

What is Quantitative Easing?

Quantitative Easing is the practice of the central bank purchasing government bonds from the private sector in order to grow the size of its balance sheet. Within a monetary system that uses bank reserves (such as the United States), these purchases create excess reserves within the banking system. (In the "Simplified Framework" for government finance introduced in Chapter 3 of *Understanding Government Finance*, such a policy could not be implemented, as settlement balances are assumed to remain at zero.)

This is supposed to affect the economy as the result of two mechanisms.

Quantity Theory of Money. Since bank reserves are considered part of the monetary base, this policy would be considered inflationary by those who believe in the Quantity Theory of Money. They will act on those expectations, and use money to buy goods and services that they believe will rise in price.

Supply effects. By reducing the amount of bonds outstanding, the average maturity of government debt falls, and this reduction in the supply will raise the price of bonds (which lowers long-term interest rates). Lowering long-term rates makes borrowing more attractive, which allegedly will boost economic growth.

The first mechanism – the Quantity Theory of Money – is frankly disreputable. In its simplest form, the theory says that if we double the amount of money in an economy, and hold all else equal, the price level will double. This theory has a long history within economics, and there are many within the financial markets who strongly believe in it. Central bank economists supposedly did not believe in it, but they were happy to prey upon the gullibility of the believers. The Quantity Theory of Money (and variants) is discussed elsewhere within this text.

The second mechanism – the reduction of supply – appears more plausible. I am something of a fundamentalist in my belief that expectations determine bond yields (as discussed in Appendix A.3 of *Understanding Government Finance*), but I am willing to concede that a large enough binge of buying by the central bank can lower bond yields. The Bank of Japan engineered such a squeeze in the markets in 2014-2015. That said, the effect does not appear to be significant relative to the variability of rate expectations. Quantitative Easing was effective more as a signalling device: if the Fed is buying bonds, that is a sign that they will not hike rates any time soon. This drops yields by lowering the expected path of short-term rates.

Measuring the effectiveness of the reduction of supply is also be-devilled by the issue that the central bank purchases are not the only thing that affects the maturity structure of government debt. The Trea-sury can modify the weighted average of debt outstanding by changing its issuance patterns. Yet I have never seen a convincing study that re-lates the weighted average maturity of government debt to bond yields.

There was a wave of studies by economists in the private sector and central banks "proving" that the Fed's Quantitative Easing policies low-ered bond yields by very specific amounts. However, none of the arti-cles that I read controlled for the pattern of issuance by the Treasury. And guess what: the Treasury lengthened the maturity of the debt it auc-tioned, largely cancelling out the effect of Fed purchases. Ignoring this effect is particularly embarrassing, as the consensus was that a similar policy – "Operation Twist," undertaken in the 1960s – failed precisely because the Treasury lengthened the maturity of the debt it auctioned.[8]

"Qualitative Easing" Does Work

There is a variant of Quantitative Easing that is useful – Qualitative Eas-ing. When a central bank engages in *Qualitative Easing*, it is buying (or lend-ing against) risky assets (normally bonds) from the private sector. This does have the side effect of growing the central bank's balance sheet, but that is incidental.

The effect of qualitative easing is to reduce the supply of risk assets that are under price pressure. Existing holders of bonds who doubt the viability of the issuer will be given a chance to exit, which means that those holders will no longer be putting downward pressure on the bonds in the secondary market. (If an issuer's bonds are collapsing in price in the sec-ondary market, it is extremely unlikely that they will be able to secure new financing from anyone other than distressed debt specialists – who are go-ing to offer extremely unattractive financing terms.) This will make it much easier for the entities that issued the risky assets to roll over their debts, and hence reduce the odds of a bankruptcy due to illiquidity.

---

8   For a discussion, see the box "Operation Twist Revisited" on page 45 of the BIS Quarterly Review, June 2009. URL: http://www.bis.org/publ/qtrpdf/r_qt0906.pdf

This is a form of government direct lending, which is industrial policy. It is a reasonable way of dealing with an irrational seizure in risk assets. (For a longer discussion of such lending, see "Central Banks as Pawnbrokers," Section 16.)

The initial Federal Reserve interventions during the Financial Crisis took the form of Qualitative Easing, and it seems reasonable to believe that they were an important factor in stabilising the financial system. (Those purchases were controversial, particularly amongst those who wished to see the financial system pay for its shenanigans before the crisis.)

Otherwise, Qualitative Easing is really the explanation for the success of European Central Bank bond market interventions. Since there is no central fiscal agency, there are no pan-euro risk-free assets (although people treat German Bunds as such). European Central Bank purchases of non-core government bonds helped stabilise spreads, and thus kept the financial strains on governments (outside Greece) under control. Since those are "government" bonds, many commentators do not distinguish these purchases from Quantitative Easing, which is a misleading slippage in terminology.

Part III Monetary Controversies

7 Instability of Money Velocity

This article is largely new, but portions are based on the article "When Does the Quantity Theory of Money Make Sense?" October 25, 2014.

Money would be an extremely useful economic indicator if the velocity of money were stable. In that case, the growth rate of the monetary aggregate would match the growth rate of nominal GDP. *(The definition of the velocity of money is found in "Primer: Money Neutrality and Velocity," Section 5.)*

This essay looks at some historical experiences of the United States and Canada. In summary, the velocity of some monetary aggregates was stable for periods of time, but this was not generally the case.

My analysis here is graphic: I show figures of velocity over a long time interval, and let my readers draw their own conclusions. There is a good reason why I prefer to leave the discussion qualitative. My argument is that the velocity of money is unstable, and has little predictive power. However, a determined analyst could presumably find that money velocity could be predicted as a function of other economic variables. It is essentially impossible to prove that no such technique exists.

Currency in Circulation

The narrowest definition of money we could use is currency – notes and coins in circulation. This aggregate is not usually looked at, but it has some interesting properties.

Figure 3 on page 32 shows the relationship between currency and nominal GDP in Canada. The top panel shows the velocity of circulation for currency (nominal GDP divided by currency outstanding). The bottom panel shows the inverse of the ratio, which is currency as a percentage of GDP.

As will be seen, the relationship between currency and nominal GDP in Canada has been relatively stable. (There is a ripple in the time series, as currency holdings vary on a seasonal basis.) Since 1980, currency holdings have stayed within a narrow band around 3-3.5% of GDP.

Although currency in circulation is not normally considered a monetary aggregate, in Canada it is now very close to the monetary base (M0). Canada

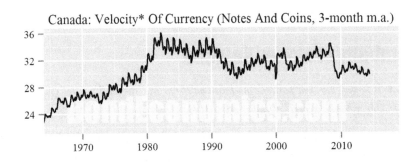

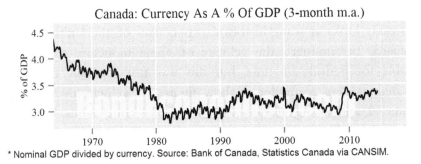

* Nominal GDP divided by currency. Source: Bank of Canada, Statistics Canada via CANSIM.

Figure 3. *Canadian GDP and currency in circulation.*

abolished the need for bank reserves (bank settlement balances held at the central bank), and so the other major components of the monetary base are quite small. Therefore, we might expect the velocity of the monetary base going forward to be similarly stable to the past history for the velocity of currency.

The long-term stability of Canadian currency velocity is not universal. Figure 4 on page 33 shows the equivalent time series for the United States. We see that there are obvious trends in the time series, indicating that there is a gap between the growth rate of the stock of currency and GDP. For example, the currency stock has been rising as a percentage of GDP since 1990. The usual interpretation of the money supply growing faster than GDP is that "inflationary pressures" have been building up, and that the inflation rate will catch up to the growth rate of money. However, this situation has persisted for almost three decades, and many serious commentators have been more worried about deflation than runaway inflation.

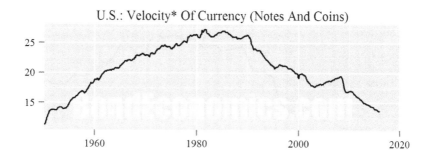

* Nominal GDP divided by currency. Source: Fed Board of Governors, BEA (via FRED).

Figure 4. *U.S. GDP and currency in circulation.*

The instability of American currency velocity is embarrassing for believers in a stable velocity. I picked a time series from the CANSIM database in a somewhat random fashion, and compared the stability of its velocity to that of the U.S. currency aggregate.

Figure 5 on page 34 shows the velocity of U.S. GDP based on Canadian mink production. As the bottom panel shows, Canadian mink production velocity has been more stable than the velocity of U.S. currency over the post-1990 period. If U.S. currency in circulation has less predictive power about nominal GDP than a somewhat random Canadian time series over a span of two and a half decades, it is hard to see the predictive value of monetary aggregates. (Unless the series is not random – inflation is always and everywhere a *mink* phenomenon!)

It is unsurprising that currency in circulation is a relatively stable fraction of nominal GDP. Households and businesses have relatively settled patterns for dealing with currency, and the amount of currency held is go-

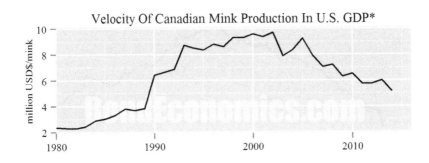

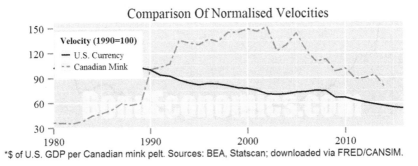

*\$ of U.S. GDP per Canadian mink pelt. Sources: BEA, Statscan; downloaded via FRED/CANSIM.

Figure 5. *Comparison of normalised velocities of money and mink.*

ing to be related to nominal incomes (and nominal Gross Domestic Product is equal to nominal Gross Domestic Income – within measurement errors). The currency outstanding aggregate is more likely to have a stable velocity than other monetary aggregates, since it is not the amalgamation of financial instruments with different characteristics.

However, even if currency velocity is stable, it is of no use for economic analysis.

1. If we are solely interested in making forecasts, we have replaced the task of forecasting nominal GDP with the task of forecasting the currency in circulation (and changes in velocity). It is unclear that this is an easier forecasting exercise.

2. Unlike the monetary base (which largely corresponds to the size of the central bank's balance sheet), currency in circulation is not under the direct control of the central bank. As discussed in Section 4.2 of *Understanding Government Finance*, the government's role in the determination of currency outstanding is pas-

sive – it is largely determined by how much currency is withdrawn by bank customers (and holdings in bank vaults).

The second point is the reason why currency in circulation was ignored as a monetary aggregate. Since it was not under the control of the central bank, the Monetarist prescription of a fixed growth rate of the money supply was meaningless. As a result, the focus was on monetary aggregates that the central bank could presumably control. These are discussed in the following sections.

My assertion that the central bank cannot control money in circulation might be disputed. One possible argument is that the central bank could somehow drop currency from helicopters – a literal "helicopter drop" – and increase currency in circulation. Even if we ignore the fact that such a step would be an illegal breach of the mandate of the central bank, the currency would just return to the banking system almost immediately. The second argument is more complex. One could take an economic model in which we *assume* that the central bank has direct control over the level of national income (GDP). The model also *assumes* that there is a tight mathematical linkage between nominal income and currency holding. We then use the model to show that since the central bank controls nominal income, it also controls the stock of currency in circulation. The response to such an argument is straightforward – if you take a mathematical model that assumes that your view is correct, the model will always support your viewpoint. However, that tells us nothing about how the real world operates.

The Monetary Base

When we move to the wider monetary aggregates, velocity has been less stable over time. The smallest aggregate normally considered is the monetary base. The most important components of the monetary base are currency in circulation, and the deposits of private banks at the central bank. If we ignore other items (such as the Federal Government's deposit at the central bank), the monetary base roughly matches the size of the central bank's balance sheet. Since the central bank can always go out and buy assets in order to expand its balance sheet, we can view the monetary base as being under the control of the central bank. (Post-Keynesians would argue that this apparent control is illusionary, but that is another issue.)

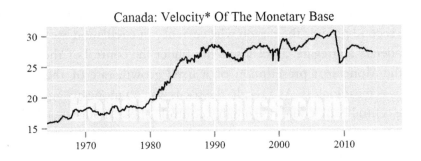

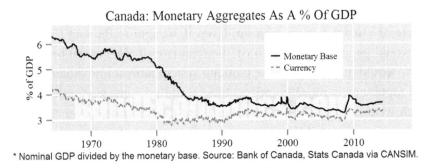

* Nominal GDP divided by the monetary base. Source: Bank of Canada, Stats Canada via CANSIM.

Figure 6. *Canadian monetary base and GDP.*

Figure 6 depicts the data for the Canadian monetary base. We see that the monetary base converges towards the more stable currency in circulation figures, which is a result of the abolition of bank reserve requirements. The net result is that the velocity for the monetary base has a large structural break.

However, in other countries, central banks did a very good job of testing the importance of the monetary base. As shown above, post-Financial Crisis purchases of bonds by the Federal Reserve ("quantitative easing") led to the explosion of the monetary base from around 5% to over 20% of GDP.

Despite the rampant growth of the monetary base, the inflation rate has been extremely stable (Figure 8 on page 38). The core CPI inflation rate (the rate of inflation when we exclude volatile energy and food prices) has not deviated much from around 2%, which is slightly lower than it was during previous expansions.

Other countries have also launched massive expansions of their central bank balance sheets, without any impact on inflation. Japan started its cen-

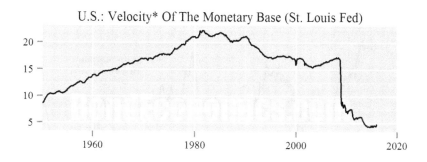

U.S.: Velocity* Of The Monetary Base (St. Louis Fed)

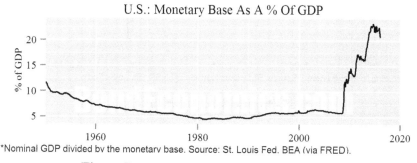

U.S.: Monetary Base As A % Of GDP

*Nominal GDP divided by the monetary base. Source: St. Louis Fed. BEA (via FRED).

Figure 7. *American monetary base and GDP.*

tral bank expansion even earlier, yet the price level has been largely stable over this period (with inflation alternating between mild inflation and deflation).

Wider Aggregates

Once we start looking at wider monetary aggregates (such as M1, M2, and M3), the aggregate no longer is under the direct control of the central bank.

The definition of the various monetary aggregates varies by country, as banking practices differ. For the United States, M1 and M2 are defined as follows in the Federal Reserve H.6 Release:[9]

- **M1.** "M1 consists of (1) currency outside the U.S. Treasury, Federal Reserve Banks, and the vaults of depository institutions; (2) traveler's checks of nonbank issuers; (3) demand deposits at commercial banks (excluding those amounts held by depository

---

9   Board of Governors of the Federal Reserve, H.6 Release – Money Stock Measures. URL: https://www.federalreserve.gov/releases/h6/current/default.htm

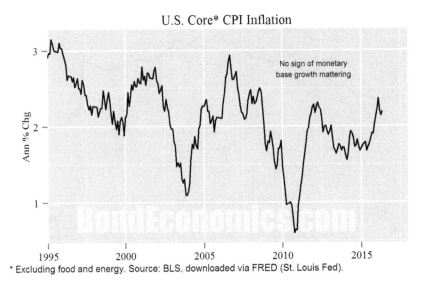

Figure 8. *U.S. core inflation.*

institutions, the U.S. government, and foreign banks and official institutions) less cash items in the process of collection and Federal Reserve float; and (4) other checkable deposits (OCDs), consisting of negotiable order of withdrawal (NOW) and automatic transfer service (ATS) accounts at depository institutions, credit union share draft accounts, and demand deposits at thrift institutions."

- **M2.** "M2 consists of M1 plus (1) savings deposits (including money market deposit accounts); (2) small-denomination time deposits (time deposits in amounts of less than $100,000), less individual retirement account (IRA) and Keogh balances at depository institutions; and (3) balances in retail money market mutual funds, less IRA and Keogh balances at money market mutual funds."

(The Federal Reserve used to calculate a wider aggregate – M3 – but this was suspended because of cuts to the statistics budget. The disappearance of M3 provided a great deal of entertainment, as it resulted in conspiracy theories that suggested the move was undertaken because the United States was on the verge of hyperinflation.)

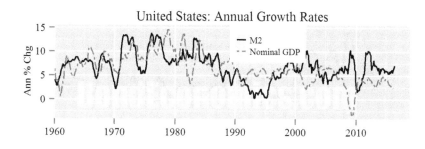

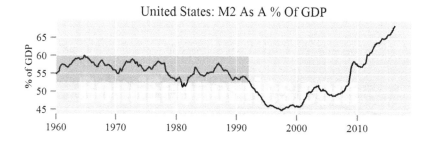

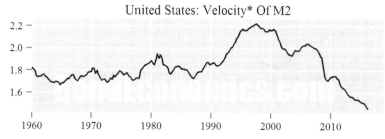

*Nominal GDP divided bv M2. Source: Fed. BEA. downloaded via FRED.

Figure 9. *Behaviour of U.S. M2.*

Figure 9 shows the relationship between M2 and nominal GDP in the United States. The top panel shows annual growth rates, which are only loosely related. The middle panel shows M2 as a percentage of GDP (the inverse of velocity), and we do see that it was relatively stable during 1960-1982, mainly staying within the range of 52.5%-60% of GDP (highlighted region).

If M2 as a percentage of GDP stayed within that range, then we would have a relatively strong relationship between their growth rates. For example, if annual M2 growth was running 2% more than annual GDP growth, we know that this outperformance would end within at most seven years –

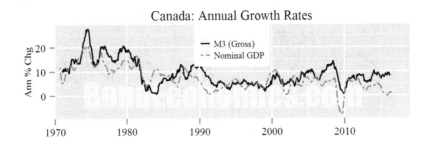

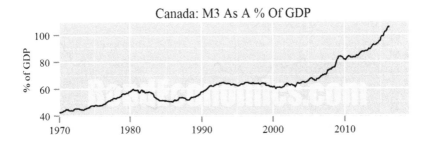

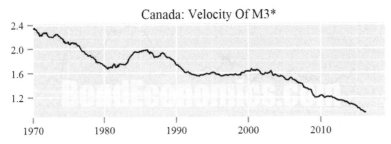

*Nominal GDP divided by M3. Source: Bank of Canada. Statistics Canada via CANSIM.

Figure 10. *Behaviour of M3 in Canada.*

since the ratio would move outside the range.

Sadly for the usefulness of M2, it subsequently moved out of that range, and displayed much greater variability. For example, M2 growth has outstripped nominal GDP growth almost continuously since the year 2000 (that is, almost two decades), yet there is no sign of nominal GDP "catching up."

If we turn to Canadian data, Figure 10 shows that the velocity of M3 has been completely unstable since 1970. M3 has steadily grown at a faster rate than nominal GDP. Although some might view this as a sign of building inflationary pressures, it needs to be viewed in the context of the trends of all financial assets. The ratio of the stock of almost any financial asset relative to GDP has been rising over recent decades. These trends are the result of policy choices as well as economic forces (demographics, inequality) that have caused the private sector to stockpile financial assets.

Concluding Remarks

It is possible to find some periods of time in which the velocity of money is somewhat stable. However, as my facetious mink example shows, many time series exhibit a stable ratio to GDP over sample periods. In order to be useful, we have to have good reason to forecast that the ratio will be stable going forward. Past history shows that this has not been the case for monetary aggregates.

8 Should We Care About Money Supply Growth?

This essay has not been published in this format, but the charts were referred to in "Is High Money Growth Telling Us Anything?" November 20, 2016.

Although money should not be accorded special status within economic theory, this does not mean monetary aggregates by themselves are useless as economic indicators. There are reasons to expect that "money numbers" are going to be a relatively good quality economic indicator, particularly in countries where national statistics are weak. This was certainly the case during the initial decades after World War II, when macroeconomic statistics measurements were in their infancy. (This can explain why older economists might pay more attention to money numbers.)

This essay follows up "Instability of Money Velocity," Section 7. The difference between the analysis in that section and the previous is that the focus here is upon growth rates of money and nominal GDP, while velocity is an attempt to relate the level of the money stock to nominal GDP. We could

Figure 11. *U.S. M2 and GDP growth 2010-*

imagine a situation where velocity is unstable (for any number of reasons), yet we can still draw conclusions from periods of "high" or "low" growth in monetary aggregates. In technical terms, we could hope that there is a correlation between money growth and nominal income growth (or inflation).

For example, Figure 11 on page 43 depicts the growth rates of the M2 monetary aggregate and nominal GDP for the United States at the time of writing. It would be quite easy to look at the chart, and tell a story that inflationary risks are building up because of too-easy Federal Reserve policies.

The rest of this essay discusses why I am skeptical about drawing such a conclusion from the money numbers alone (*please see the disclaimer in the next paragraph*), even though there were periods in which rapid money supply growth did appear to contain useful information. When we look at longer runs of data, we find that money growth can decouple from other data, and so apparent predictive successes at any particular point could be chalked up to luck.

(*As an aside, I do not currently disagree with the message of M2 growth at the end of 2016. Although I am not particularly bullish on nominal GDP growth, it is likely to pick up from its current subdued pace because of mean reversion. Furthermore, it appears likely that the new Republican administration will enact tax cuts, and so there should be a fiscal expansion in 2017.*)

Advantages of Monetary Aggregates as Data

The beauty of the narrow monetary aggregates is that they are based on highly centralised instruments, and they are (almost by definition) easy to value. The components are either central government liabilities (which are tracked by the central government for obvious reasons), or bank deposit data that are tracked by bank regulators.

The advantage due to centralisation starts to break down once we start looking at wider monetary aggregates. Those aggregates include instruments such as money fund holdings or repos. Assuming the data are available, they are more difficult to assemble, and we would have greater concerns about the quality of the data. (Is the financial sector creating functionally similar products outside the sight of regulators?)

The technical advantages of money versus other economic variables that result from this centralisation and the simplicity of the data include the following points.

- Data can be collected at a higher frequency (weekly instead of monthly or quarterly).
- The lag in data publication can be much reduced.
- The data do not depend upon the manipulation of raw data, such as is required by price index or production data.
- The data generally do not need to be revised.

There are only a few disadvantages with the data, but they mainly revolve around attempts to create generic monetary aggregates that are comparable across countries. The instruments that are included in each aggregate (for example, M2 versus M1) vary, and are not strictly comparable between different regions. Changes in financial practices will mean that there may be structural breaks in behaviour. (This partly explains why economists who focus on money keep inventing new adjustments to the money numbers.)

These technical advantages are allied to some of the theoretical advantages of money. Broad money aggregates include instruments that are created by the act of borrowing. Any realistic analysis of a monetary economy tells us that nominal income growth is going to be at least correlated with increased debt levels. (One needs to be careful about this; the "multiplier" between increased debt levels and nominal income growth should not be expected to be stable.) Even though I am skeptical about money as a theoretical concept, it does give us a partial glimpse into the trends of debt creation, and the data are available in a timely manner.

However, this advantage of timeliness only matters if you are attempting to time the economic cycle at a high frequency – an extremely difficult task. The broad debt statistics that are available in a less timely manner (for example, from the Flow of Funds report) give a much better global overview of financing trends. My view is that we need to have a good idea of the current situation before we worry about trying to get a one-month lead on the rest of the market. Given that it took *years* for the consensus to grasp the slow nature of growth in the current cycle, I am not particularly concerned about a 1- to 2-month delay to get data that are more reliable. However, if a country lacks a reliable Flow of Funds report, monetary aggregates may be the only information that is available.

Money Growth Itself Should Not be the Concern

I am assuming here that we are not concerned about the money growth numbers by themselves, rather their effect on the economy. This is an assumption that is not shared by some of the more money-centric analysis frameworks; this section discusses this divergence.

Firstly, if a country has some form of currency peg system (such as a Gold Standard), and if the money supply is growing faster than the country's holdings of the backing commodity (gold holdings), then the backing ratio will decline. This raises the odds of a speculative attack on the currency. This is a very real concern for historical analysis, but is not applicable to modern free-floating currencies.

Secondly, some Austrian economists define "inflation" to be money growth, and argue that everyone who calls rising consumer prices inflation is using the term incorrectly. I would argue that this is a misunderstanding of how languages operate – if everyone except you uses a word in a certain fashion, *you* are the one who does not understand the contemporary definition of the word.

In any event, even if we redefine the term inflation to be money supply growth, it is unclear why we should care about it. Central banks are typically not just given mandates to target generic "inflation," their mandates are defined in terms of the movement in a particular consumer price index. The Austrian argument appears to rely on the Quantity Theory of Money, which would imply a constant velocity (which I discussed in the previous section).

Finally, Monetarists enjoy characterising monetary policy in terms of the rate of growth of the money supply. They argue that only unsophisticated bumpkins define monetary policy in terms of the level of interest rates. I disagree, as I believe that the central cannot set the level of the money supply. (This is the endogenous/exogenous money debate that is discussed in Section 10.) However, even if we grant the Monetarists a terminological victory and define monetary policy in terms of money growth, that does not tell us about the linkage between monetary policy and other economic variables. Once again, the object in this essay is to discuss such linkages.

OK, But Does Money Analysis Work in Practice?

Although I am open to believing that money growth data could be useful for analysing the economy, I have not found any convincing means to do so. By itself, that is meaningless – my inability to find any useful relationship may just reflect a lack of imagination. That said, if there were investors who did find reliable relationships, we would expect (using market efficiency arguments) that the release of monetary data would move markets. We have not seen such behaviour since the 1980s.

There are a number of ways in which money growth could be useful for forecasting other economic variables (for example, price indices or nominal GDP). I list possibilities in order of their analytical strength.

1. There is a strong relationship between the levels of money growth and the target economic variable. (The strongest possible relationship would be if "velocity" were constant.)

2. The level relationship is imperfect, but there is a correlation between money growth and the target variable, with money leading the other variable. For example, this means that if money growth accelerates, we will expect the other variable to start rising within a few months – although we might not be able to guess the magnitude of the rise of the target.

3. Money growth and the target variable are correlated, but money growth is essentially coincident with the other variable. Although this might not appear to be useful in theory, it is helpful in practice, given the reduced publication lag of money supply numbers.

4. You can throw money growth numbers in with other variables into a multiple regression blender and get a model to estimate the target variable.

The rest of this essay examines the U.S. historical experience during most of the post-war era, looking at the linkage between money growth and nominal GDP growth. The analysis is visual, that is, the data are displayed graphically. Although academics may scoff at just eyeballing charts, such a presentation is probably less misleading than regurgitating the results of statistical tests.

Firstly, I do not think there is a reliable statistical link between money growth and nominal GDP growth. However, statistical tests can only determine if a particular relationship between variables is statistically significant (over a sample period). If I find tests that confirm my position (that there is no relationship), all I have done is to test a particular rule relating the variables. It may be that I have just missed another rule that is statistically significant, possibly as the result of my analytical biases. Secondly, I have seen a lot of dubious results "proved" statistically; looking at the actual data in chart form, and understanding the context, is a necessary step. (An example is the relationship between government debt levels and growth, which I discuss in the next section.)

U.S. Experience: Early Post-War

The analysis here uses the monetary aggregate data that has been adjusted by the St. Louis Federal Reserve Bank staff. The earliest period examined is from 1948-1960, for which only the monetary base is available.

The early post-war era saw a deep recession in 1948-1949, which was the result of demobilisation after World War II. That period was unusual, as the economy was transitioning from a command economy that was managed almost solely with an eye on the war effort. As a result, we should be cautious about drawing conclusions

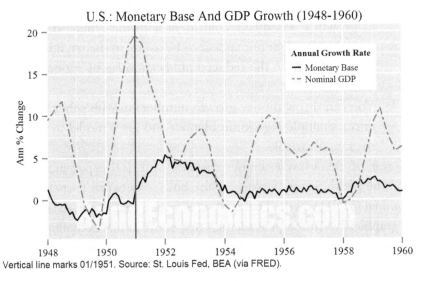

Figure 12. *U.S. monetary base and GDP growth (1948-1960).*

from data for that era. (For example, one of the dubious statistical attempts to prove that high government debt levels reduced growth levels was entirely based upon that singular recession, which coincided with the high government debt levels of the immediate post-war era.)

Therefore, I would not put too much emphasis on the utter disconnect between nominal GDP growth and the growth rate of the monetary base that occurred in early 1951. At the point marked by the vertical line, nominal GDP growth actually peaked close to 20%, while the level of the monetary base was essentially stagnant. Subsequently, the growth rate in the monetary base accelerated while nominal GDP decelerated. Given my previous caution about this era's data, all we can say is that there is no stable mechanical link between money supply growth and nominal GDP growth.

In the later parts of the sample period (post-1954), one might detect a correlation between the growth rate of the monetary base and nominal GDP growth. The growth rates were markedly different, which presumably reflects the transition away from the conditions of wartime finance. If one refers back to the charts in "Instability of Money Velocity" (Section 7), there was a trend decline in the velocity of money in this period.

U.S. Experience: The Monetarist Period

During the period from 1960 to 1980 the data looked like what Monetarists predicted it would. (As I discussed in "Instability of Money Velocity," the true end of stable velocity was even later, around 1992. However, the sample period was cut down to two decades in order to make it easier for readers to examine the data.)

Figure 13 on page 50 shows the growth rates for the monetary base and nominal GDP for the period 1960-1980. There appears to be a strong correlation between the growth rates. However, the relationship is not perfect; for example, the growth rates diverged strongly in early 1976 (marked with a vertical line).

However, there are reasons to be suspicious of the monetary base as an indicator, as it misses innovations in financial practices. We would expect more success with a wider monetary aggregate. The figure below shows M2 growth, and it appears to have a better fit; in particular, it does not have the divergence that took place in 1976 (also marked with a vertical line). The preferred measure was M3, but the Federal Reserve stopped calculat-

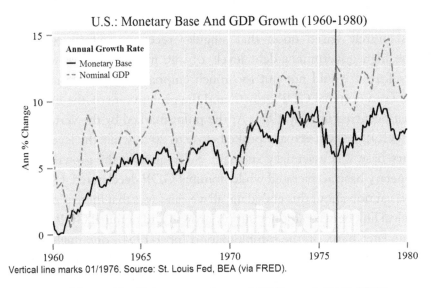

Figure 13. *U.S. monetary base and GDP growth (1960-1980).*

ing it as a result of statistical budget cutbacks (which provided fodder for the believers in the Quantity Theory of Money who are also partial to suspicions of the motivations of government agencies).

However, switching monetary aggregates was not able to save money

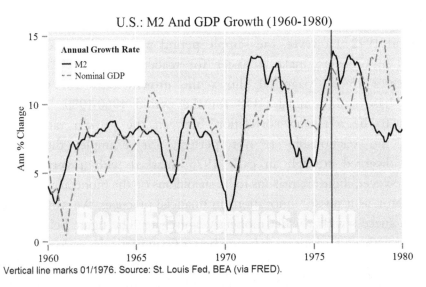

Figure 14. *U.S. M2 and GDP growth (1960-1980).*

growth as an indicator over a longer time span, as discussed in the next section.

Recent U.S. Experience

This historical survey ends with the period from 1980 to 2007. (The period from the Financial Crisis to the present is deliberately ignored, as quantitative easing greatly affected the monetary aggregates, without having much of an impact on the economy. Since the argument in this essay is that money growth is supposed to be an indicator that naturally reflects economic activity – and not that the money supply can be set by central banks to achieve policy targets – this manipulation of the data by policymakers can be legitimately ignored.)

The choice of 1980 as a dividing line for periods was arbitrary, and as previously noted, money growth had almost as good a track record in the early 1980s as in the 1960-1980 interval. However, the experience in the mid-1980s was dubious, unless one takes the line that there can be very long lags between changes in money supply growth and the economy. The vertical line (marking February 1987) highlights the divergence that opened up between nominal GDP growth and money supply growth. The previously mentioned "long and variable lag" story is not particularly help-

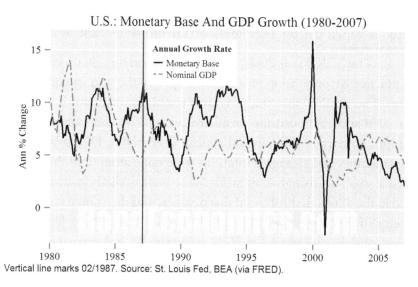

Figure 15. *U.S. monetary base and GDP growth (1980-2007).*

ful when we have continuous business cycle oscillations (as was the case before the long expansions that started in the 1990s) – all sinusoidal signals of the same frequency can be viewed as either leading or lagging each other.

Once we hit the 1990s, it would be hard to see how changes in base money could have been viewed as predicting anything. The growth rate was accelerating from late 1989 until the 1990-91 recession hit, and thus was moving in exactly the wrong direction.

Furthermore, it is hard to square the rapid monetary base growth of the post-recession period with the tepid nominal GDP growth rates, and it lagged behind the acceleration seen during the late-1990s telecom boom.

The experience during the 2000s was similarly weak. The base grew rapidly during the weak post-recession period, while it was decelerating during the 2003-2005 period when the housing bubble was building up steam.

Finally, the monetary base "blew up" as an indicator around the year 2000. Federal Reserve Chairman Alan Greenspan bought into the story that the "Y2K bug"[10] put the financial system at risk, and the Fed "flooded the system with liquidity" to forestall the risks. Once New Year 1999 passed, the Fed returned its balance sheet back to its usual size, creating the trailing downward spike. Many commentators blamed the final blow off in the tech stock bubble – that peaked in March 2000 – on the Fed's overreaction to the Y2K bug. (My feeling is that the stock market bubble had its own momentum, and Fed policy could do little to deflect it.) Once again, erratic policy decisions wiped out the usefulness of the monetary base as an indicator.

---

10   The Y2K (Year 2000) bug referred to errors that were caused by the practice of only using two digits to specify the year in computer programs. The result is that the programs could not distinguish between the year 2000 and 1900, causing problems because of date comparisons. For example, January 1, 2000, would appear to be before December 31, 1999. Since memory and storage limitations were quite strict until the 1990s, this practice was surprisingly common. Many banks relied on software developed in the 1960s that followed this practice, and the source code for these systems often disappeared. The result was that there was a feeding frenzy by consultants specialising in Y2K conversions, and some people feared that the integrity of the banking system would be damaged by these errors. However, the New Year rollover was highly anticipated, and no major documented problems happened on the rollover.

Figure 16. *U.S. M2 and GDP growth (1980-2007).*

Turning to M2, it was possibly even less reliable than the monetary base as an indicator during this sample period. The growth rate in M2 matched the behaviour of the monetary base in 1987, also diverging from GDP growth then (marked with a vertical line).

During the early 1990s expansion, M2 growth was essentially dead. Although it was a weak expansion, the economy was still growing. Money growth started to catch up with economic growth in the post-1995 period, but then shot off in the other direction – expanding very quickly during the weak growth period after the 2001 recession.

In summary, it was impossible to make any useful economic forecasts using money growth as an indicator during the post-1990 period. In fact, it was almost more effective as a contrary indicator (predicting the opposite of what will happen).

I started working in finance in 1998, and the completely erratic behaviour of the money supply as an indicator had been apparent for some time. My experience was that only a few diehard Monetarists would quote the money growth numbers, while everyone else dropped those charts from their chart packs.

Concluding Remarks

My analysis here was relatively brief and qualitative, and it would certainly be possible to look at the experience of other regions. It is entirely possible that money growth is a reliable indicator elsewhere. That is not contradicted by the experience in the United States that I examined here – it worked in the United States relatively well from 1960 to 1980 (at least). The problem is that you face the same risk as the Monetarists in the 1990s – you have no idea when it will stop working as an indicator.

It might be possible to change the definition of the money supply used, or apply some transformations to create a reliable indicator. (I tried doing that earlier in my career, and failed to do so.) However, you once again run into the same problem – your new series might work on historical data, but we need to wait years (if not decades) to see if it holds up against new data.

9 Seriously, Money Is Not a Zero-Coupon Perpetual

This essay first appeared on BondEconomics.com on July 24, 2016; some additions and changes have been made.

The excessive importance accorded to money within economic theory makes it the source of sloppy arguments. For example, some people equate it to a "zero-coupon perpetual bond." Perpetual zero-coupon bonds have long been a punch line in financial market humour; such a product is definitely not like money.

This article discusses how fixed income instruments are priced, and portions of the text may be difficult for some readers. However, the article was popular amongst my readers with a more technical background, and so I left the text complexity unchanged.

Background

A perpetual bond is a bond that pays a fixed coupon on a fixed schedule (for example, annually, or semi-annually), but has no fixed maturity date. For example, we could have a perpetual bond that pays $1 on every December 1st (with the standard correction for weekends). These show up a lot in financial and economic theory, but are rare in practice. (The British government issued perpetual bonds called *consols. Consol* is often used as a synonym for *perpetual,* since it sounds cool.)

It should be noted that companies issue perpetual preferred shares that look like consols, but their valuation is skewed by the fact that they are relatively junior in the capital structure of the issuer. Their value depends upon interest rates, modified by the uncertainty about the long-term survival of their issuer. (There also may be embedded options.)

Valuation

If a perpetual bond does not have any embedded options, and there is no default risk (see below), we can scale the face value/coupon by any amount, without it affecting the return characteristics of the bond. For example, the following two ownership structures exhibit the exact same cash flows:

- holding perpetual bonds with a face value of $100 and a 2%

annual coupon,
- holding perpetual bonds with a face value of $200 and a 1% annual coupon.

In both cases, the holdings pay $2 per year, and there are no other possible cash flows. We are indifferent to either characterisation of the bond, and so we would not object to a scaling that keeps our annual cash flows unchanged. (If there is a default, the face value would presumably matter for recovery calculations; and I discuss the issue of embedded options below.)

The usual convention in mathematical finance is to assume that consols pay $1 per year, and there is a notional 1% coupon. This works fine if the issuer manages to auction the bond at a 1% yield; otherwise, the issuer is auctioning the bond away from a par value. Since these bonds tend to appear only in mathematical models, the institutional problems associated with auctioning bonds away from par do not affect analysis. Therefore, we can treat the bond as having the 1% coupon, and the auction price reflects the bond yield.

For such a standard structure, if we are conveniently pricing the bond on the coupon date (ex-coupon), the pricing formula is: $p = 1/r$, with p being the dollar price, and r the quoted yield.

Examples:
- If $r = 0.01$ (1%), $p = $100.
- If $r = 0.005$ (0.5%), $p = $200.

It can be seen that the price tends to infinity as the quoted yield goes to zero. This well-known relationship has caused some commentators to make incorrect claims about bond market duration as bond yields went to zero; for finite maturity bonds, the maturity date caps the Macaulay duration of the bond. (The price sensitivity of a bond, such as the modified duration, is close to the Macaulay duration, but does not have the convenient units that are comparable to a maturity date.)

Embedded Put Option

Some bonds have an embedded put option (redemption option) – owners of the bond can demand immediate payment on the bond ahead of maturity (following some contractual limitations).

This turns the bond valuation into an exciting exercise in fixed income derivative pricing. I do not want to go into that subject; instead, I will give a lower bound for the value of the bond.

If we have an embedded put option, we have a possible cash flow that is not a coupon payment. In this case, the face value matters.

We will assume the perpetual is described by:
- $100 face value.
- 1% annual coupon.
- Puttable to the issuer (the government) at par ($100) on any coupon date (after the owner receives the coupon). (On non-coupon days, the bond is puttable at a price that takes into account accrued interest on the coupon. My analysis here ignores that issue; the time axis only considers annual coupon dates.)
- No default risk (standard assumption for risk-free rate curves).

Since this bond has an embedded option, we cannot easily relate its price to a risk-free yield curve (where there are no embedded options). In order to make the discussion more easily understood, we will assume that the government also issued a non-puttable perpetual bond.

If the non-puttable bond trades at a yield of r, it can be easily shown that the lower bond of the price of a $100 face value puttable bond is:
- $100, if $r > 0.01$;
- $1/r$, otherwise. (Note: this is greater than $100.)

(Why this holds: we know that the embedded option gives the holder of the puttable bonds greater rights than the option-free consol. Therefore, its price is at least equal to the option-free bond. Meanwhile, we know that it can always be exchanged for $100, so that creates a floor price.)

If the volatility of interest rates is non-zero, the value of the bond with the embedded option is going to be greater than the lower bound given above. The extra value is the "time value" of the perpetual (American) put option. (The option value would be greatest near the strike of the redemption option, which is at $r=1\%$.)

What matters for this floor price is the redemption value of the bond. The standard convention would be that the bond is puttable at par, *and this will not be affected by changes in the coupon rate.* (In the real world, finite maturity puttable bonds will have varying redemption prices, which typically only start some years after issuance. Pricing such bonds requires the use of numerical techniques.)

Money – A Zero-Coupon Puttable Perpetual

We can now see how the argument that money is a zero-coupon perpetual goes wrong.

The usual argument that money is a zero-coupon perpetual bond would look roughly like this. We take a sequence of instruments, where the coupon as a percentage of face value declines. We can return to the standard 1% coupon formulation, but it relies on dividing by the coupon rate. It is not hard to see that setting the coupon rate to zero would cause problems in the definition of the option-free instrument.

This is not the case for a puttable perpetual. It always has a floor value of 100% of face, regardless of the coupon. Setting the coupon rate to zero just ensures that the value remains at 100% of face: there is no upside to the bond price – assuming rational market pricing, and that interest rates are positive. (If nominal interest rates are negative, you would rather own a zero coupon puttable perpetual than its face value of the monetary instruments with a negative interest rate, and so the market price would be above $100.)

Is money puttable? Yes it is. You can redeem it for face value to meet tax obligations. You cannot do this with a bond. (This is under normal circumstances; one can imagine an issuing government allowing taxpayers to pay taxes by returning its bonds to the issuer. Such a policy would create a similar price floor for the affected bonds.) The money instrument cancels out the tax obligation at a 1:1 ratio. If you wanted to meet a tax obligation with a bond, you would have to sell it, and there is no guarantee that you can sell it at its face value.

Moreover, this logic can be extended to other obligations that are not due to taxes, such as debts, or regular payments such as rents. There are laws that ensure that various forms of "money" (currency, bank deposits) trade at par with each other (this was not always the case). You can use any of these forms of "money" to meet those private-sector obligations. (Some instruments in wide "monetary aggregates" do not necessarily trade at par, such as the discount instruments held by money market funds.)

Even if you do not personally pay taxes (such as the case of "you" being a pension fund), you just need to find somebody who does. You would be a sucker to sell your monetary instrument at below face value to such an entity, since you know how that entity would value it.

Money With Interest

An additional wrinkle is that money as it typically appears in economic models pays 0% interest. This is because writers have currency (notes
and coins) in mind when talking about "money." In the real world,
there are many financial instruments that are part of "monetary aggregates" (since money-fixated economists need to keep patching the aggregates), so there are "monetary" instruments that do indeed pay interest. (For example, the Federal Reserve currently pays interest on
excess reserves, and those reserves are part of the "monetary base.")

For this section, I will discuss currency, which does not pay interest.

Although currency pays no interest, banks can exchange currency for settlement balances ("reserves") at the central bank at par. If
those settlement balances pay a rate of interest, we can view them
as a perpetual floating rate instrument. Such an instrument could
be theoretically swapped into a fixed-rate instrument, and so has
non-zero value (since the swaps have a net present value of zero).

Since the central bank must redeem currency for settlement balances, we can see that currency has a redemption conversion option into a perpetual floating-rate security.

(If the central bank does not pay interest on settlement balances, the
argument is slightly more complex. If the central bank wants to keep
the short-term rate at a positive level, it has no choice but to drain the
excess reserves by replacing them with interest-bearing instruments.)

How Does Money Price Versus Real Stuff?

The discussion above was purely a fixed income pricing argument, where we
are reducing future cash flows to their "Net Present Value." Since the Net
Present Value is expressed in units of "money," and $1 of "money" has a
Net Present Value of $1 *by definition*, we obviously have to end up with a re-
sult that money has a stable par value. When we price fixed-income instruments, we just view future (expected) cash flows as being "forward money,"
and we are comparing the value of "forward money" versus "spot money."

This just tells us that fixed income pricing of default-risk-free instruments forms a closed system. It does not tell us about the value of money
versus goods and services in the real world (that is, the price level). What

determines the price level depends upon your economic belief system. (Once again demonstrating that a degree in anthropology is probably more useful for understanding economic discussion than a degree in economics.)

- If you believe that mainstream economics is even slightly close to correct, and if you follow the chain of mathematics, you end up with the Fiscal Theory of the Price Level. The punchy summary of the Fiscal Theory of the Price Level is that expected fiscal surpluses (that is, taxes) drive the price level (also known as the value of money).

- If you are a post-Keynesian, what you think about this topic might depend upon your tribal affiliation. The neo-Chartalist wing (for example, Modern Monetary Theory) argues that taxes drive money, which as a verbal formulation sounds similar to the Fiscal Theory of the Price Level.

- If you are an Institutionalist, many factors ensure that money has a stable value. Contract prices are fixed, as are debt obligations. If I owe the bank $1000, and have to pay back that loan by the end of the day, $1000 has a very real value to me. There are rules that ensure that various forms of "money" trade at affixed par value amongst each other. If those rules are suspended, then we can see different forms of money swinging in value versus each other. A cheque written against an insolvent bank is not worth a lot in the absence of deposit insurance and cheque-clearing regulations.

- I have a hard time characterising other schools of thought. For example, some Austrians dispute the very existence of the concept of a price level.

In any event, saying that the value of money is driven by taxes ties in exactly with the redemption option discussed above.

Concluding Remarks

Demoting money to just another financial instrument helps us to avoid walking into traps like trying to treat it as a zero-coupon perpetual. Instead of discussing a mystical abstraction, we can sit down and try to price the actual instrument that appears in the economy.

10 Primer: Endogenous Versus Exogenous Money

This essay appeared on BondEconomics.com on September 25, 2016.

One of the long-running debates within economics is the question whether money is *endogenous* or *exogenous*. Those who follow internet economic debates can expect this argument to flare up periodically. This debate should largely be considered dead and buried; and abolishing money from economic theory would put the final nail in the coffin.

This essay takes a narrow view of the debate; does the central bank set the level of the "money supply" or does it set an interest rate? Some authors take a wider definition of what constitutes the "endogenous money debate," but I view those to be separate questions. These wider definitions are more relevant to understanding recent macro arguments. These general definitions are more abstract, relying on unmeasurable concepts like the expected money supply. Since the assertions in those debates cannot be compared to empirical results, there is no way of resolving them one way or another.

Exogenous Versus Endogenous

This an old debate (described below), and the exact terms of debate have changed over time. Since I believe that the debate is over, I will not worry about the exact phrasings used historically, and offer a simplified explanation.

- The "money supply" is *exogenous* if we believe that it is set directly by the central bank; private agents within the economy will set interest rates on instruments in response to the supply of money. (*Exo-* is the Greek root that indicates that something is external; in this case, the money supply is set externally to the model of the private sector.)

- The "money supply" is *endogenous* if we believe that the central bank sets the policy rate of interest; the level of money is determined by factors within the private sector. (The root *endo-* implies that it is an internal property; that is, the level of the money supply is determined within the model of the private sector.)

It seems straightforward to determine which view is correct: just ask the central bank what it is doing! As noted in Section 4.1.1 ("Endogenous Money to the Forefront") in Marc Lavoie's *Post-Keynesian Economics: New Foundations*,[11] central banks in the modern era (post-1990, say) are more transparent in how they operate, and so they give the answer: the money supply is endogenous.

For example, take the discussion in the paper "Money Creation in the Modern Economy" (a working paper by Bank of England researchers McLeah, Radia and Thomas).[12]

> *Neither step in that story [exogenous monetary base and a money multiplier] represents an accurate description of the relationship between money and monetary policy in the modern economy. Central banks do not typically choose a quantity of reserves to bring about the desired short-term interest rate. Rather, they focus on prices — setting interest rates [emphasis in original – BR].*

Previously, central banks kept their operations veiled in opacity. Furthermore, during the early 1980s, they announced that they were following the Monetarist policy of forcing the money supply to grow at a target rate. (Monetarist economists had been the primary believers in exogenous money, a view that has been absorbed by many in the mainstream, even those that do not consider themselves Monetarist.)

Killing "Money" In Economic Theory Kills Exogenous Money

If we follow my prescription of abolishing "money" from economic theory, the debate is even easier to deal with. Instead of discussing whether the central bank can set some nebulously defined "money supply," we have to ask ourselves: can the central bank set the level of the stock of various instruments?

- There is no mechanism for the central bank to set the level of

---

11   *Post-Keynesian Economics: New Foundations*, Marc Lavoie, Edward Elgar Publishing Limited, 2014. ISBN 978-1-78347-582-7. The section referred to is found on pages 182-183.

12   "Money creation in the modern economy," by Michael McLeay, Amar Radia and Ryland Thomas, Bank of England Quarterly Bulletin, 2014 Q1. URL: http://www.bankofengland.co.uk/publications/Documents/quarterlybulletin/2014/qb14q1prereleasemoneycreation.pdf

currency in circulation. It cannot force people to withdraw currency from banks. It could attempt to stop people from doing so (by stopping the delivery of new currency to banks), but this would trigger something resembling a bank run, and so the financial stability mandate of central banks would prevent that action.

- Loans are created voluntarily within the private sector, in response to economic conditions. There is normally no mechanism to force banks to increase lending (which creates deposits), although the central bank could attempt to reduce growth rates by imposing quantitative limits on credit growth. In modern economies, credit rationing has been eliminated, so this no longer applies. *(In other words, in an economy with effective quantitative credit controls, exogenous money might be viewed as correct. That said, Hyman Minsky's analysis of the evolution of the post-war banking system in the United States underlined the extreme difficulty of enforcing financial regulations like quantitative credit controls outside of an emergency.)*

- Since deposit growth is not controlled by the central bank, required reserves are also outside of their control. (See comment below.)

- The only real freedom of action the central bank has is to buy assets (or lend against assets) so as to create excess reserves within the system. This allows the central bank to grow its balance sheet relative to a certain minimum size (currency in circulation plus required reserves), but that minimum size is still determined by private sector actions. (This was made apparent by the policy of Quantitative Easing.)

The situation regarding reserve balances can be complicated by the reality that the central bank operates by buying and selling assets (or using loans) to hit its interest rate target. The argument here is that the central bank uses the price signal of the interbank interest rate to guide its actions, and does not really care about the magnitude of its operations. This is illustrated in Figure 17 on page 64, which depicts the behaviour of reserve balances during 1959-2000 (which is before the Federal Reserve lost its marbles and instituted Quantitative Easing).

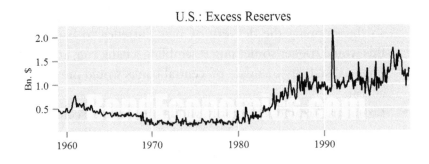

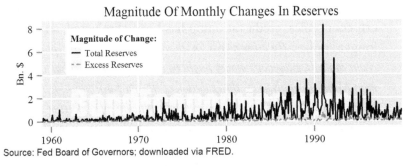

Source: Fed Board of Governors; downloaded via FRED.

Figure 17. *Excess reserves in the United States, and volume changes.*

The top panel shows the level of excess reserves in the United States banking system during that era. Up until the mid-1980s, it was well below $1 billion. Although $1 billion is a lot of money for an individual, that amount is minuscule relative to required reserves. The bottom panel shows the magnitude (that is, absolute value) of monthly changes in total reserves as well as the changes in required reserves. The monthly changes in total reserves dwarfed that of excess reserves. Since excess reserves were essentially a small constant amount, the Federal Reserve had essentially no discretion in the reserves it supplied each month. Notably, this was also true for the early 1980s, which was when the Federal Reserve was allegedly targeting the money supply (see below).

In summary, the policy-making committee at the central bank sets a target level (or target range) for the interbank rate, and the open market desk injects/drains reserves until the market rate of interest hits the target level (range). (Historically, the Federal Reserve allowed for a relatively wide variation around the target rate; once banks grew accustomed to the framework of an explicitly announced policy rate, the market rate was very tightly tied to the target.) The open market desk had very little leeway in setting the magnitude of the operations, since they had to provide enough reserves to cover required reserves, plus the small excess.

One could try to claim that the money supply is influenced by central bank policy; but the same thing is allegedly true of the price level when the bank targets inflation.[13] Nobody sensible believes that the central bank has the power to set the price level in the economy to whatever level it wishes each month (which is what a belief in an exogenous price level/inflation rate would imply).

Historical Background

The previously cited text by Marc Lavoie gives a background to this monetary debate. In Section 4.1.2, he notes that this idea could be traced back to the debate between the Currency School and the Banking School in England in the early nineteenth century.

> *Ricardo and the Currency School argued that only coins and Bank of England notes could be considered as money, that this stock of money determines aggregate demand, and that aggregate money determined the price level, thus giving support to the quantity theory of money.*[14]

The Banking School position was that the situation was more complicated in that bank deposits were involved.

The debate flared up during the hearings of the Radcliffe Commission in the late 1950s. Entertainingly enough, academics refused to listen to testimony of central bankers, under the theory that people who do something all day still know less about their area of expertise than academic economists. *(Interest rate strategists are well acquainted with this phenomenon.)*

Lavoie argues that the post-Keynesian view was still not that much different from the mainstream, at least until the 1970s – when the Monetarist

---

13   Purists who think in terms of continuous time economic models would object that this would only be true for price level targeting, and not inflation targeting. However, in the real world, the inflation rate is defined relative to the fixed level from a year before, and so inflation targeting is equivalent to price level targeting in the near run.

14   Page 184 of *Post-Keynesian Economics: New Foundations*, Marc Lavoie, Edward Elgar Publishing Ltd., 2014. ISBN 978-1-78347-582-7.

fad regarding "money supply targeting" took hold. (I discuss that episode below.)

Outside of the scattered remnants of Monetarism, there really is not a lot of support for exogenous money. Most mainstream economists interpret their models in terms of the central bank setting the rate of interest. However, the picture is muddied by the relatively simple money demand equations that exist. (In many models, there is no term that forces a demand for money, and so the models predict zero money holdings when interest rates are positive. In such a model, the money supply is obviously endogenous, since the central bank has no means whatsoever to change its level.) From a mathematical perspective, there exists an invertible function that relates interest rates to the money supply. Therefore, we can specify a "reaction function" for the central bank either as a rule on interest rates or as a rule on money supply growth. As a result, using those models, one could argue either way regarding whether the money supply is endogenous. The issue is what happens when some extra complexities are introduced into the model, which would break the symmetry between specifying monetary policy in terms of interest rates or the level of the money stock. As my discussion notes, the analysis of how the various instruments are used within the economy in the real world breaks that symmetry.

The Monetarist Experiment

Monetarists argued that the central banks should control the growth of the money supply, following the logic of the Quantity Theory of Money. This position was translated into a belief that the central bank operated by setting the quantity of "money" in the economy. Various countries experimented with money supply targeting, including Canada (in the 1970s), the United Kingdom (until the early 1970s), and the Volcker Fed. (I am less familiar with the German Bundesbank's experience, which I believe was more successful than the cases I discuss here. The Bundesbank was the only central bank that paid much attention to money growth when I started my career in finance in the late 1990s. This translated into the early European Central Bank discussing M3 growth, but attention to that aggregate has waned as the euro area turned to the more urgent question of not allowing the common currency to disintegrate.)

There is extensive literature on how money supply targeting worked in practice. However, I was unable to find a modern reference that greatly differs from my characterisation above: the central bank set the interest rate so that money growth would be near some target level.

One good example is the Bank of Canada working paper "The Quantity of Money and Monetary Policy," by David Laidler,[15] where he writes:

> *Simplifying somewhat, but without misrepresenting the essence of the case: a money-demand function was estimated using monthly data; values of its real income and price level arguments over a rather short policy horizon were forecast and plugged in, along with the lagged values dictated by the econometrics of an equation based on monthly data; a target value for the money supply became the equation's left-hand-side variable; the resulting expression was solved for the value of the interest rate that would set money demand moving towards that target value over some desired time horizon; and the Bank then set its interest rate instrument at that value.*

His paper covers the Canadian experience, but there were strong parallels to the situations in the United States and the United Kingdom, but perhaps not Germany. The article is an interesting reference for my purposes, since the author was relatively sympathetic to the objectives of the money supply targeting regime. (He also positions the debate in a somewhat different fashion than I do here, which makes the discussion more nuanced.) In the article, he states:

> *In light of this evidence, the widely held view that money-growth targeting was a failure is a little too pat. This is not to deny that genuine problems of interpreting the behaviour of M1, the aggregate on which the experiment focused, arose during the course of money-growth targeting, particularly from late 1979 onwards, or that these problems raised important doubts, still relevant today, about the usefulness of monetary aggregates as policy guides. It is, however, to question the common interpretation of this earlier episode, namely that it demonstrates a degree of inherent unreliability in these variables that should disqualify them from anything but a subordinate position in policy formation.*

I admit to a bias against the use of monetary aggregates in analysis, but I have no strong reason to believe that they are useless. Like other credit aggregates, they should provide some information about the evolution of the economy; however, the behaviour is dependent upon the current in-

---

15   "The Quantity of Money and Monetary Policy," by David Laidler, *Bank of Canada Working Paper 99-5*, April, 1999. URL: http://www. bankofcanada.ca/wp-content/uploads/2010/05/wp99-5.pdf

stitutional framework. In other words, the usefulness of monetary aggregates in analysis is an empirical question.

Concluding Remarks

The debate between endogenous and exogenous money is one that would have been resolved a long time ago if economic theory did not assume the existence of some magical entity called "money" within its models, and instead confined itself to the analysis of the instruments that appear in the real world. Although the historical debate covered more territory than I discuss here, the most interesting part can be dealt with by accepting that the central bank sets the rate of interest, and the "money supply" is determined by the reaction of the private sector to macroeconomic developments.

11 The Incoherence of Money Neutrality

This essay has not been previously published.

Money neutrality is a concept that has attracted controversy in post-Keynesian economics, but it seems to be a non-interesting topic. I actually see very little practical difference between the Monetarist position – the *bête noir* of post-Keynesian economics – and a standard post-Keynesian view (the idea of a stock-flow norm), *once we accept that money is endogenous.* Money neutrality is only a source of debate if the two disputants are on the opposite sides of the exogenous-endogenous money debate. *(I discuss that debate in the previous essay – "Primer: Endogenous Versus Exogenous Money.")* An argument about money neutrality is a waste of time, as we need to focus on the true underlying issue (money endogeneity).

How (Not?) to Define Money Neutrality

The problem with money neutrality is how it is defined. The intuitive version is that if the money supply increases and all else is held equal, then all that happens is that prices increase proportionally to the change in money, and "real values" (quantities of output, hours worked, etc.) are unchanged.

The problem with this standard "all else equal" (*ceteris paribus* for people who want to sound sophisticated) phrasing is hand-waving. We need a more formal definition before we discuss the idea; as otherwise, we end up debating our own personal definitions of what that phrasing means.

I grabbed the text *Monetary Economics: Theory and Policy* by Bennett T. McCallum off my bookshelf, and looked up the definition of money neutrality.[16]

Within Section 5.6, he discusses what he refers to as the "Classical Model." Money neutrality is defined in two parts (on page 95).

- "The other experiment that we consider at present is that of an exogenous, policy-induced increase in the stock of money from M^0 to M^1."
- "In the new equilibrium, then, the values of $y, r, n, W/P, \text{ and } M/P$

16   Bennett T. McCallum, *Monetary Economics: Theory and Policy,* Macmillan Publishing Company, 1989.

are the same as before the increase in M. It follows that the values of P *[the price level]* and W *[wages]* must have risen in proportion to M, for otherwise either W/P or M/P would have changed. In short, the increase in the money stock changes all nominal variables in the same proportion and results in no change in any of the real variables. This property of the system is referred to as money neutrality. In the classic model, in other words, we have a case of the *neutrality of money* [emphasis in the original]."

Some might argue the above phrasing is just a long-winded way of writing out "increase the money supply, holding all else equal." Not so; the key is that we need to specify how the money supply changes in the first place.

Furthermore, the model discussed did not have a well-defined concept of time. We can extend the definition of money neutrality to *short-run* and *long-run* neutrality.

- If *money is neutral in the short run*, the mathematical relationships described above will hold over all time periods (no matter how short).
- If *money is neutral in the long run*, the above mathematical relationships may not hold over short periods of time, but the time series tend to converge to the predicted values.

I think it would be safe to say that almost nobody believes that money is neutral in the short term (as that would imply that velocity is constant, which is obviously wrong to anyone with access to time series data). However, the argument of Monetarists was that money was neutral in the long run.

What makes this definition useless when talking about real-world economies is that it assumes that "money" is exogenous; it is an external variable set at an arbitrary level by policy makers. *This definition is meaningless in a model where the money supply is endogenous.* We need to find some other definition, which ends up having important practical differences.

I have seen a lot of post-Keynesians object to the notion of long-run money neutrality, presumably because that is what the Monetarists believed. However, entering into that argument based on this definition requires accepting that money is exogenous – which runs counter to post-Keynesian doctrine. Since this definition does not apply to real-world economies, it makes no sense to argue whether it is true or not.

Neutral Endogenous Money?

I am unaware of any attempt to define money neutrality when the money supply is endogenous. However, it is clear that it is very difficult to do so.

Since the level of money is determined by the model and the exogenous variables, we are in a position that we cannot hold "all else equal": we must change an exogenous variable in order to change the money stock within the model economy.

We could attempt to use the following definition.

(Failed Definition) *Fix two scenarios that are defined by two differing sets of exogenous variables. Money is neutral if the real variables within the economy always converge to the same levels, while the level of money can be different in the two scenarios.*

This definition fails because it is rather obvious that we can find scenarios in which real variables will obviously converge towards different levels. Examples:

- If one scenario were that the country involved launches a nuclear war that annihilates all life on Earth, one might expect that economic output would be somewhat lower than the case where war was avoided.

- If the two scenarios involved the government taxing 20% of GDP versus 90% of GDP (note that taxes are imposed in real terms), supply side economists would insist that total output would be lower in the high tax case.

In other words, we cannot allow for any possible changes to exogenous variables.

I can think of two reasonable replacements for money neutrality that appears to capture the intent of the idea.

1. **Interest rate neutrality**. Shifting the expected path of the policy rate by a fixed amount does not have a long-term effect on real variables.

2. **Inflation target neutrality**. Assuming that we are in an inflation-targeting regime, changing the inflation target level does not have a long-term effect on real variables.

These definitions are presumably closer to what the Monetarists believed, but the changes raise awkward questions.

In the first case, why do we care about monetary policy if it has no real effects? Do we really believe that it is impossible for a central bank to cause a recession by pursuing a policy of ultra-high interest rates? Moreover, from the perspective of a mainstream economist, it is hard see how we can permanently change the level of interest rates without changing something else. If the central bank's reaction function resembles something like a Taylor Rule, such a change would end up being equivalent to changing the inflation target (the second case).[17]

The second possibility appears more plausible. For example, would we expect greater long-term Canadian prosperity if the target inflation rate is 3% instead of 2%?[18]

Even if a small change in the inflation target did matter, we have no ability to know what the exact outcome would be, and so we end up with presumed "inflation neutrality" because of our ignorance. Of course, there are presumably limits – a sustained inflation rate of 10% might lead to quite different economic outcomes than 3%. (The theory being that there is a psychological aversion to "high" rates of inflation, and people waste resources on strategies designed to protect themselves from it.)

Velocity and Money Neutrality

One possibility is to express long-run money neutrality in terms of ve-

17   Technically, we could shift the interest rate generated by a Taylor Rule by changing the real interest rate term within the equation to a different value from the model's natural real rate of interest. However, the net result would be a persistent miss of the inflation target, and so is mathematically equivalent to a change in the inflation target while using the correct natural rate of interest.

18   Some theories suggest that there would be a difference. Mainstream economists are currently excited about the zero lower bound for interest rates, and raising the inflation target would allegedly lower the risk of the policy rate hitting 0%. Alternatively, many post-Keynesians invoke *Verdoorn's Law,* which I would summarise as: greater short-term growth increases long-term growth rates, since businesses will invest more, raising productivity. Although reasonable, it is also possible that raising the inflation target could just raise inflation expectations (and administered prices) without affecting real variables

locity: that is, the velocity of money tends to revert towards some "equilibrium" or "steady state" value. This seems to be equivalent to what is wanted for money neutrality: if one scenario results in having double the money supply of the other, nominal GDP would also be double.

Such behaviour is predicted by some Stock-Flow Consistent (SFC) models. The argument is that economic actors tend to want to hold financial assets near target levels that are some multiple of their nominal incomes. (This is known as a stock-flow norm, as the desired level for the stock of financial assets is a multiple of the flow of nominal income.) As a result, the ratios of stocks of financial asset divided by nominal GDP typically tend towards steady state values. In the case of money, this ratio is the reciprocal of the velocity of money, and hence the velocity converges towards a steady state value.

Since this is just a restatement of a stock-flow norm, it is unclear why "money neutrality" should be privileged as a special theoretical concept.

Concluding Remarks

Once we accept that the level of money balances is determined by private sector behaviour, it is nearly impossible to come up with a satisfactory definition for money neutrality. The concept is purely an artifact of the mistaken classical view that the money supply is exogenous.

12 Would Eliminating Money From Monetarism Have Stopped It From Jumping the Shark?

This essay has not been previously published.

Old School Monetarism is a classic example of an economic theory running into problems because of a focus on money (or jumping the shark, as I prefer to phrase it). I picked up a copy of the 1992 edition of *Monetary Mischief* by Milton Friedman, and I was frankly impressed by the clarity of his thinking when compared to modern mainstream macro. However, analytical problems within the text revolved around his fixation on money.

I will be note that there is a contemporary offshoot of Monetarism – Market Monetarism. The analysis in Market Monetarism is more complex, and my impression is that the new school of thought has covered up the obvious weaknesses of old school Monetarism. However, the discussion of Market Monetarism is beyond the scope of this essay.

Folk History of Old School Monetarist Monetary Base Targeting

I am only interested in one aspect of Monetarism herein: the constant money growth rule. The way that this rule was popularly understood was that the central bank ensured that the "money supply" grew at some fixed rate (3% a year, say). In this case, the economy would grow steadily with a low, steady rate of inflation. This idea grew politically popular during the high-inflation 1970s, and finally led central banks to attempt to target the growth of the money supply. The side effect was that interest rates exploded higher, the developed world had some nasty recessions, and central banks discovered that they could not actually control money supply growth as a result of financial innovations (banks found means to structure their affairs so that they held less reserves). The idea of monetary base targeting was shelved, and central banks went back to what they did before – setting a policy rate of interest. (The target level for that interest rate was not actually announced in the United States until the 1990s.)

Since the constant money growth rule failed as a policy instrument, Monetarism lost a great deal of popularity. Although some might dispute the idea that Monetarism "failed," it would be hard to dispute that Monetarism "jumped the shark"[19] as result of the experiments in money supply targeting.

It should be noted that the constant money growth rule ("the $k\%$ rule") was not the sole theoretical insight of Monetarism, as summarised by Bennett T. McCallum in an online economic encyclopedia:[20]

> *Friedman's constant-money-growth rule, rather than other equally funda-mental aspects of monetarism, attracted the most attention, thereby detracting from the understanding and appreciation of monetarism. In particular, this led to the comparative neglect of Friedman's crucial "accelerationist" or "natu-ral-rate" hypothesis, according to which there is no long-run trade-off between inflation and unemployment; that is, the long-run [P]hillips curve is vertical.*

As a post-Keynesian, I am not a huge fan of Milton Friedman's other contributions to economics, while mainstream economists would be more sympathetic. That said, my thesis is that if he dropped his focus on the money supply, his reputation amongst mainstream economists would have been greatly improved. That is, dropping money from Monetarism would have improved it (at least from the perspective of mainstream macro).

Friedman's Analysis – Mostly Plausible

Post-Keynesians enjoy pointing out that the Monetarist experiment in monetary base targeting in the early 1980s failed. (For example, L. Randall Wray dismisses the "faddish Monetarist policy of controlling inflation by controlling base money" as a failure in one paragraph.[21]) (I discuss why the policy would not work in "Primer: Endogenous versus Exogenous Money" – Section 10.) Although Monetarists might dispute that money

---

19   "Jumping the shark" refers to an incident in North American popular culture. The exact meaning is somewhat ambiguous, but it implies that a particular incident acts as a signal that something that was previously popular lost its way.

20   Bennett T. McCallum, *The Concise Encyclopedia of Economics: Monetarism*, URL: http://www.econlib.org/library/Enc/Monetarism.html

21   L. Randall Wray, *Modern Money Theory: A Primer on Macroeconomics for Sovereign Monetary Systems*, Palgrave Macmillan, 2012, ISBN 978-0-230-36889-7. The quotation is found on page 80 within Chapter 3.

supply targeting was a failure, it is clear that the policy did not work the way Monetarists predicted. In my view, this makes the pre-1980 Monetarist literature only of interest to economic historians (or connoisseurs of human folly). Correspondingly, for my research, I was most interested in looking at the (old school) Monetarist analysis that was published after the money supply experiments were attempted. In this essay, I discuss Milton Friedman's analysis in *Money Mischief: Episodes in Monetary History.*[22] This book is aimed at a mass audience, which is useful to my purposes. I was not interested in the theoretical nuances that are featured in academic works; rather, I wanted to see how Friedman explained his views in plain language.

Friedman's book is much clearer than modern mainstream macroeconomics. However, the analysis failed at a few key points – in places where he discussed the role of money in the economy.

In Chapter 8, in the section "Why the Excessive Money Growth?" (page 205 in my edition), Friedman writes:

> In the United States, the accelerated monetary growth from the mid-1960s to the end of the 1970s – the most recent period of accelerating inflation – occurred for three related reasons: first, the rapid growth of government spending; second, the government's full employment policy; third, a mistaken policy pursued by the Federal Reserve System.

Other than the third reason (mistaken policy by the Federal Reserve System; discussed below), I would find it hard to disagree with him. I would paraphrase his first two reasons using terminology taken from post-Keynesian economics:

1. Central government deficit spending is the major driver of inflation. (This is Functional Finance.)
2. The "full employment" policies implemented in the 1970s created a bias towards inflationary outcomes. (Exactly what Hyman Minsky argued at the time.)
3. The structure of government financial operations is such that deficit spending creates growth in government debt outstanding, as well as the monetary base. (This is the Modern Monetary Theory analysis.)
4. In the long run, households try to keep money holdings steady

22   Milton Friedman, *Money Mischief: Episodes in Monetary History,* Harcourt Brace Jovanovich, 1992. ISBN 0-15-162042-3.

as a percentage of their income. (He defines "real cash balances" as being measured in units of time, which is how many weeks of wages cash holdings represent [page 20]). As a result, money holdings tend to revert towards steady state levels in the long term. (This is the concept of a stock-flow norm from Stock-Flow Consistent modelling.)

I will immediately note that if you are an economics student, arguing that Milton Friedman was really just a post-Keynesian is a guaranteed way to get an 'F' in a course given by almost any professor. There is a political chasm between Monetarists and post-Keynesians, and the mathematical models each prefers are distinct. That said, all of the simple mathematical models used by economists have a poor fit to real-world data. However, I would note that the way in which Friedman explained how his models were supposed to work is very similar to the descriptions of post-Keynesians of their models (outside of the discussion of money, as discussed below).

The clarity of Milton Friedman's description of how inflation operates is in deep contrast to the analysis within contemporary mainstream macro. In modern macro models, nominal quantities largely snap to where the central bank wants them to be. There is no way of relating that fantasy to real-world behaviour; it only makes sense in models where this central bank power is just assumed to exist.

Money Led Friedman Astray

The following passage (on page 208) pretty much sums up the problems with old school Monetarism.

> *The third source of higher monetary growth in the United States was a mistaken policy of the Federal Reserve System. <u>The Fed has the power to control the quantity of money</u> [emphasis mine – BR], and it gives lip service to that objective. But it acts a little like Demetrius, in Shakespeare's A Midsummer Night's Dream, when he shuns Helena, who is in love with him, to pursue Hermia, who loves another. <u>The Fed has given its heart not to controlling the quantity of money, which it can do, but to controlling interest rates, something that it does not have the power to do</u> [emphasis mine – BR]. The result has been failure on both fronts: wide swings in both money and interest rates.*

To modern ears, saying that the Fed cannot control interest rates seems particularly silly. As shown in Figure 18, the traded rate in the Federal

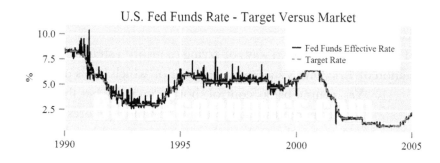

U.S. Fed Funds Rate - Target Versus Market

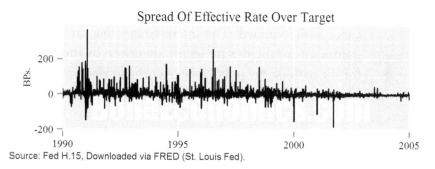

Spread Of Effective Rate Over Target

Source: Fed H.15, Downloaded via FRED (St. Louis Fed).

Figure 18. *Effective Fed Funds rate versus target.*

Funds market tracked the policy target closely in the post-2001 period (at least until the Quantitative Easing episode). Before 1995, the target level for Federal funds was not announced, so that the idea may have been more plausible then.[23] During 1998-2001, there was still a gap between the target and the effective funds rate; the central bank operations desk viewed its mandate as stabilising the moving average of the market rate near target.

Once Quantitative Easing was announced, the Federal Reserve was only able to keep the market rate within a target band, as there were technical fators that led to a divergence between various short-term interest

23   Previously, the Fed announced the discount rate, but there is a reluctance by banks to borrow from the discount window, and so there was a gap between that rate and market interbank rates. In 1995, the Fed announced the target for the federal funds rate, in order to close that gap. See page 3 of "The Implementation of Monetary Policy," *The Federal Reserve System: Purposes & Functions*. Washington, D.C.: Federal Reserve Board. URL: http://www.federalreserve.gov/pf/pdf/pf_3.pdf

rates. Although control over short-term rates was not exact, the central
bank can keep it within a range that would be considered tight by any reasonable observer.

There appear to be two ways of trying to justify a straightforward interpretation of Friedman's statements; neither of which holds up to scrutiny.

1. Yes, central banks control short-term rates, but they cannot af-
    fect term interest rates. Such an argument ignores the historical
    reality that the Federal Reserve did control bond yields in the
    early post-World War II era (and the Bank of Japan has started
    a policy of capping bond yields at the time of writing). Further-
    more, this is a misunderstanding of how the government yield
    curve is determined. The interest rates that are economically
    significant for the private sector are driven by the expectations
    for the path of the policy rate over the medium term.

2. The central bank has an inflation target, and in order to hit
    that target, cannot set interest rates at arbitrary levels. This is
    a reasonable position; whether you should think it applies de-
    pends upon your views about the relationship between interest
    rates and other economic variables. (If you think the economy
    is highly sensitive to interest rates, the central bank cannot de-
    part too far from the "correct" level without missing its infla-
    tion target. Conversely, if you believe that interest rates have no
    effect on the economy, the central bank can set the policy rate
    wherever it wishes without affecting anything.) In any event, if
    you take this line, the exact same logic applies to the level of
    money within the economy. For those of us with an interest in
    arcane academic debates about interest rates, this is an enter-
    taining discussion, but it offers us limited insight into the actual
    behaviour of the central bank.

Abolishing money from economic theory would likely have saved
Friedman from making this rather obvious error (and the related error
involving the $k\%$ growth rule). If the base money aggregate has no special
properties, he would have put no effort in deciding whether the central
bank could control its growth, and would certainly not have decided that
trying to keep it growing at $k\%$ per year would prove anything.

"Inflation Is Always and Everywhere a Monetary Phenomenon"

The conclusion of Chapter 2 of *Money Mischief* runs through the chain of logic that leads to Friedman's conclusion that "inflation is always and everywhere a monetary phenomenon."

From one standpoint, the statement is true by definition. It makes no sense to define a "price level" in a non-monetary economy. Inflation is a sustained change in the price level; therefore, it can only be seen in a money-using economy. However, statements that are true by definition tell us nothing.

Therefore, we need to change the statement to a version that is not true by definition. One possibility: "inflation is always and everywhere the result of rapid "money" growth."

This statement can be compared to the data, and it can be refuted. The "Quantitative Easing" mania put a stake through the heart of the theory that increasing the monetary base will lead to increased inflation.

We will end up with a squishier correlation relationship, which is where Friedman's chain of logic started. "For both long and short periods, there is a consistent though not precise relation between the rate of growth of the quantity of money and the rate of growth of nominal income." (Quote found on page 47.)

However, as I discuss in "Should We Care About Money Supply Growth?" (Section 8), the relationship between the growth rates of money and nominal income is in fact unreliable. His statement may have been true based on the available data at the time, but whatever relationships existed broke down as a result of shifting patterns of finance in the economy.

Furthermore, the long-term relationship between money and nominal variables is exactly what a stock-flow consistent model predicts (and those models are definitely not driven by money growth). Since these long-term correlations are also predicted by models in which money has no special significance, they cannot be used to prove anything about the usefulness of money in economic analysis.

Once again, dropping money from Monetarism would have made its analysis more robust.

Policy Views – Open to Debate

Post-Keynesians would find a lot to object to within Friedman's book, beyond its treatment of money. Most of these disputes might be viewed as political disagreements; which side you believe is "correct" depends upon your policy preferences.

For example, Friedman emphasises the importance of inflation control, over other aspects of economic performance. This is an ancient debate, with conservatives favouring "sound money." This debate is unlikely to be resolved any time soon.

Another debate revolves around the Fed's decision to "accommodate" Federal Government spending. Friedman phrased it badly, focussing on money creation. However, if we eliminate money from the conversation, his arguments would have to take the form that the Federal Reserve should have "tightened up" monetary policy in the 1970s by raising interest rates much more rapidly than they did.

Since that is exactly what the Volcker Fed did (under the cover of pretending to hit money supply targets), and inflation did fall, this version of the argument can be viewed as correct. In fact, it is the consensus mainstream view. Many post-Keynesians disagree with that explanation of the peak in inflation rates, but that is a larger question that I cannot cover here. However, the key is that the explanation that does not rely on referring to the "money supply" is accepted by many economists.

Concluding Remarks

Abolishing money from economic theory would have converted Monetarism into some variant of mainstream economics. Although this would certainly have made it blander, it also means that it would not have jumped the shark when put into practice.

13 No, Banks Do Not Lend Reserves

This is based on an article published on June 29, 2014. That earlier version was a response to an internet debate; I have edited this version to be read without needing to refer to the other article by Professor Nick Rowe.[24] As my original noted, the disagreement with Nick Rowe might be viewed as semantic, and tangential to the points I wished to discuss. I am paraphrasing his arguments in what I refer to as the sophisticated view of reserve lending.

One of the difficulties associated with understanding banking involves the question of bank reserves. It is easy to find examples of people arguing that banks "lend out" reserves; and by implication, operations increasing reserves will allow more lending. There are two ways of justifying the theory: a simple argument or a more sophisticated one. The first is obviously wrong; the second is either wrong or meaningless. As a result, we should not link the level of bank reserves and bank lending capacity.

Simple Version

The simple version of the "banks lend reserves" argument relies on a mistaken analogy between bank lending and lending by an individual. If I lend someone $5, the usual situation is that I already have a $5 bill in my pocket, and I hand it over to the other person (in exchange for an IOU.) For a bank, the situation is assumed to be equivalent to what would happen if money consisted *only* of gold coins, and all bank deposits were backed 100% by gold coins. Figure 19 depicts how this operates. Please note that this is not a full balance sheet;

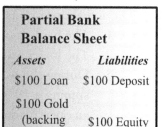

Figure 19. *Banking with gold.*

---

24   Nick Rowe, "Repeat after me: people cannot and do not 'spend' money." URL: http://worthwhile.typepad.com/worthwhile_canadian_initi/2014/06/repeat-after-me-people-cannot-and-do-not-spend-money.htm

it just shows the entries that matter for a transaction in which the bank makes a loan of $100 in a situation of full gold backing.

The transaction starts out with the bank owning $100 in gold (probably in the form of coins with a fixed face value that represents the gold parity). Since the assumption is that the bank is not acting as a fractional reserve lender, it has $100 in equity (associated with the gold asset).

When the bank makes the loan (the second partial balance sheet in the figure), it gains a new $100 asset – the loan to the customer. However, it also gains a new liability – the customer will have $100 on deposit at the bank. It needs to hold $100 in gold against that deposit, and so the $100 gold is now an encumbered asset on the balance sheet. (If we were to treat the deposit as being akin to a safety deposit box, both the deposit and gold would not appear on the bank's balance sheet; rather the amount deposited and the gold backing would only be a memo item.) The bank's equity is unchanged at $100; the equity will only change because of making a profit or loss. (If the customer repays the loan with interest, the bank makes a profit, while it would lose money if the customer defaulted. It would also make a profit from charging for deposit services.)

In summary, the bank needed some unclaimed gold before it made a loan. We can now return to the question of reserves, and try to pretend that reserves act like gold in that previous example. However, this analogy does not capture how bank finance works in practice.

The actual operations are much simpler.

1. The bank grants the borrower a loan (an asset).
2. The loan creates a corresponding deposit liability.
3. During the next reserve period, it borrows $10 in reserves (assuming a 10% reserve ratio), either from another bank, or via an open market operation from the central bank. For simplicity, the diagram assumes that liquid assets were sold to purchase the reserves; however, the bank could augment its reserves by borrowing (adding a new $10 liability to its balance sheet).

The bank just grew its balance sheet; it was not required to have reserves on its balance sheet before making the loan. Instead, it just needed to have some liquid assets, which may or may not be included in a monetary aggregate. (For example, the bank could be holding short-term government bonds.) Banks need to have excess liquidity before they enter into fractional reserve lending; the amount needed is the result of the interplay of regulations and institutional conventions. It would have been exceedingly unlikely that the liquid assets would consist of excess reserves (in the pre-Quantitative Easing era), as demonstrated in Section 10.

The final step – the bank borrowing required reserves – is of interest. We need to assume that the central bank will make reserves available during the next reserve accounting period. This assumption is justifiable under most circumstances. If a bank cannot acquire its required reserves level, it is insolvent from a regulatory point of view, which is a disastrous state to be in. (Other private sector entities would presumably find out, and flee the bank.) It would be willing to borrow reserves at an exceedingly high interest rate to avoid that outcome. This would drive the interbank rate (fed funds in the United States) above the policy rate target, and the central bank would need to undertake open market operations to return the interbank rate to target. If it refused to do so, central bank regulators would be driving segments of the banking system into insolvency because of a policy error, an act that would be extremely awkward for the central bank to justify to outraged politicians.)

Since the belief that reserves are similar to gold in a hypothetical 100% gold reserve system does not match real-world behaviour, the more interesting debate revolves around the behavioural constraints created by reserves. This is discussed in the next section.

Partial Bank Balance Sheet

Assets	Liabilities
$20 Liquid assets	$20 Equity

↓ Make Loan

Partial Bank Balance Sheet

Assets	Liabilities
$100 Loan	$100 Deposit
$20 Liquid assets	$20 Equity

↓ Borrow Reserves

Partial Bank Balance Sheet

Assets	Liabilities
$100 Loan	$100 Deposit
$10 Liquid assets	$20 Equity
$10 Reserves	

Figure 20. *Fractional reserve lending.*

The Sophisticated Version: Lending *Against* Reserves

The argument that reserves matter for lending can be paraphrased as follows. Although a bank can make a loan by just expanding its balance sheet, it needs to take into account what it expects to happen after the loan is made. It needs to hold reserves against expected losses of deposits.

The borrower is presumably borrowing to purchase something (either as an investment, or for consumption). If the bank is lucky, the seller also banks with the same bank, and the deposit liability just ends up being transferred. However, the more likely outcome is that the seller deals with a different bank and the money needs to be transferred to that bank.

Figure 21 shows the chain of transactions that are created by a bank customer transferring money to a customer of another bank. In the diagram, Customer #1 writes a $100 cheque to Customer #2; these individuals bank at Bank A and Bank B, respectively.

- Bank A's balance sheet shrinks. It loses $100 in deposit liabilities, but that is balanced by the $100 reserves it has to transfer to Bank B.
- Bank B's balance sheet expands by $100; it gains the reserves as an asset, and gains an increased deposit liability.

Therefore, a bank cannot completely ignore its reserves position – it needs to be able to deal with expected deposit losses, and those losses will increase as it increases the amount of new loans. The remainder of this essay explains why such reserve losses are of secondary importance.

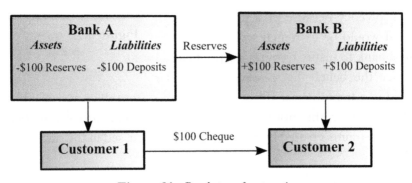

Figure 21. *Bank transfer operations.*

For simplicity, we will assume that we are discussing the banking institutions that were in place during the decades ahead of 2007 in the United States. Those conditions are not universally applicable.

1. Some countries – such as Canada – abolished bank reserve requirements, and in such cases, it is obvious that "reserves" do not matter (they do not even exist).
2. The current situation in the United States is also unusual, where there is a large excess of reserves within the system. This is discussed in the final subsection of this essay.

The discussion here ignores the issue of people withdrawing notes and coins (currency) from banks. Under normal circumstances, changes in currency outstanding is not a major issue (although there are seasonal effects, such as a lot of people taking out cash in order to go partying between Christmas and New Year's). If we follow Minsky and analyse everything as a bank, these transactions can be interpreted as depositors transferring their cash to the central bank – notes and coins can be viewed as a deposit at the central bank in bearer form. This allows us to include currency withdrawals under "deposit loss."

Liquid Assets Matter, Not Reserves in Particular

A key reason to de-emphasise reserves is that banks focus on their global liquidity position, and reserves are only one source of liquidity. If a depositor effects a transfer to another bank, the source bank can meet the cash drain by drawing on securities positions. Either an asset can be sold outright, or the bank can borrow against an asset (a repurchase transaction, typically called "repos").[25] Since banks do not want to take mark-to-market losses or gains involuntarily, they will meet liquidity needs only by selling short-term securities (for example Treasury bills), or by borrowing against assets with a relatively stable price (such as government bonds).

(A bank can also meet cash needs by borrowing in short-term money markets, but it also needs a liquid portfolio to support that borrowing.)

---

25   Within an "overdraft economy," banks do not meet liquidity needs by undertaking securities transactions; they discount loans at the central bank. This is discussed in Appendix A.2 of *Understanding Government Finance*. This text sticks with the terminology of a liquid securities portfolio for simplicity.

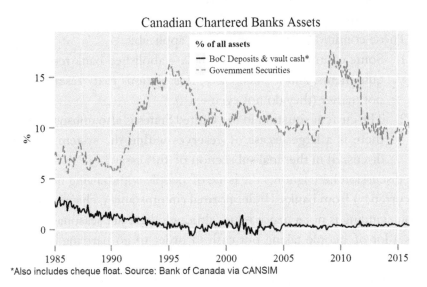

Figure 22. *Canadian bank liquid assets.*

If we look at Canadian Chartered Banks, we see that government securities (at all levels of government, not just federal government) are typically about 10% of their Canadian dollar assets (Figure 22). (Note that the Canadian banks have foreign subsidiaries, but those operations are run on a matched-currency basis. In other words, we can look at the Canadian-dollar denominated assets and liabilities in isolation.)

So why do we care about reserves in particular? I would suggest that this is because bank reserves are special because they are "money." *However, once we abolish money from economic theory, this justification disappears.* Without the privilege of special status within models, bank reserves lose their importance. Furthermore, *required* reserves are not particularly useful to banks for their liquidity management.

If we look at the U.S. system before 2007 (Figure 23), we see that excess reserves within the entire banking system were economically insignificant. Roughly speaking, the system functioned without any excess reserves. If a bank had an excess to its needs, it would lend them to banks with deficiencies in the Federal Funds market.

Even if reserves were calculated on a real-time basis (which they are not), banks still need a liquidity portfolio to deal with deposit loss.

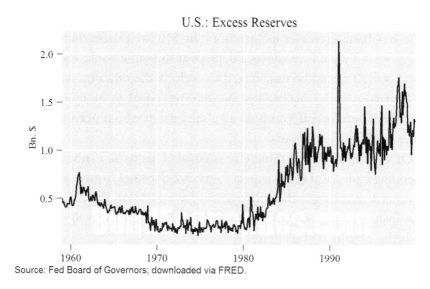

Figure 23. *Excess reserves in the United States.*

If the reserve ratio were 10% (required reserves are 10% of deposits), a $100 deposit loss only drops required reserves by $10. Although the bank could transfer $10 in reserves to the recipient bank, it still needs to raise the remaining $90 via transactions in its liquidity portfolio. (Moreover, since required reserves are not calculated in real time, it would have to raise $100 on the day of the transfer; it would only get the $10 released from required reserves in a later reserve requirement calculation.)

Since banks need other instruments to manage their liquidity needs, bank reserve positions have no way of affecting bank behaviour.

What Are the Behavioural Constraints on Banks?

It is clear that a bank cannot run down its holdings of governmental securities forever. As a result, I will now outline the practical limits for bank lending based on liquidity considerations (that is, ignoring bank capital constraints and borrower demand, which also matter).

We will examine a simple example, with the numbers chosen for ease of understanding. (If you are mathematically inclined, it is not difficult to make this example more general.) We assume that there are five private banks, and each has a 20% market share in both bank deposits and lending (and for simplicity, there is no shadow banking system). Each bank has $100 in deposits and loans. (Other items on the balance sheet balance out.)

If one bank increases its loan book by $10, we expect that:

- $2 would remain as a deposit at the same bank; and
- $2 would be transferred to each of the other banks.

That is, a bank only retains the deposits equal to its market share of deposits. Therefore, if you hold all else equal, it would need to raise $8 to cover the $10 in new loans.

Of course, not everything else is equal. This bank is not the only one extending loans, and it will expect to receive deposits from new loans made by other banks. Since the other banks have 80% of the market share of total loans, the expectation is that the bulk of new loans in the economy are being extended elsewhere.

In the simplest case, we assume that market shares in lending remain equal. By implication, every other bank also increases its loan book by $10, and then each bank would lose $8 of the new deposits. By symmetry, we see that each bank retains $2 of the loan, and loses $2 to each other bank. The net result is that no bank faces a net loss of deposits.

Of course, this example is simplified – not all banks will expand their balance sheets equally. In practice, a bank will have a loss of deposits if it is growing faster than its peers (or else its lending market share is larger than its deposit market share). The key is that the constraint is *relative*, if bank lending is generally expanding, any particular bank will be able to grow its loan book as well.

This might appear to imply that there are no constraints in coordinated bank balance sheet expansion. However, the ratio of liquid asset holdings relative to the total size of the balance sheet would drop, and so it is likely that the banks would need to raise their liquidity (somehow) to keep that ratio near target levels. But this constraint is relatively small; if liquid assets are 15% of the balance sheet, the banks would only need to raise about $1.50 (1.5% of the balance sheet) in order to keep the liquid asset ratio constant.

If the country imposes a deposit reserve requirement, required reserves will rise. However, if those reserves are not supplied, banks will be desperate for settlement balances, and bid at high prices (rates) for them. If the central bank is attempting to keep the interbank rate near a target level (which is the normal operating procedure), it has no choice but to undertake open market operations that create the reserves required by the banking system.

In summary, liquidity considerations pose only a limited constraint on aggregate credit growth; rather the constraint is on relative balance sheet expansion within the banking system.

Relationship to QE

The practical conclusion of this analysis is that Quantitative Easing (QE) will have no impact on the banking system. From the point of view of banks, it is just a change of allocation within liquid assets, and they have no additional capacity to lend.

If there is an impact from QE, it results from supply and demand factors in the yield curve. I am extremely skeptical that this matters much, at least at the front end of the curve. People price the short end of expectations, and it is nearly impossible to detect supply and demand dynamics. For example, when a central bank announces a surprise rate hike, market makers change prices immediately, without any need for securities to change hands.

Concluding Remarks

Bank reserves are only one component of a bank's liquidity portfolio. This means that central banks have very little ability to control lending growth with open market operations.

14 Money as Debt

A version of this article was first published on February 21, 2016. The original version referred to an internet debate between Eric Lonergan and L. Randall Wray. The text has been rewritten to focus on Eric Lonergan's argument that money is not debt in his book Money (Second Revised Edition).

The question of whether government-issued money is a debt has shown up in two recent contexts. The first is a fundamental argument about money, and how to think about it. The second is a more technical question: if the central bank replaces government bonds with reserves (which are a form of money), has the debt-to-GDP ratio gone down? To summarise my views: we should think of (modern) money as being some form of liability (although the semantic debate is tricky[26]). However, since the central government with a free-floating currency cannot be forced to default (as I discuss at length in *Understanding Government Finance*), one can question whether it makes sense to treat central government debt like the debt of other issuers. In particular, the debt-to-GDP ratio of such governments is essentially a piece of trivia that can be safely ignored – which implies that it does not matter whether money is included or not.

The Semantic Debate

Eric Lonergan is a fund manager, and the author of the book *Money*.[27] In the section "Introduction to the second edition," he writes:

> *A specific confusion seems to pervade formal analysis of money: this is the claim that money is a debt, or a liability, of government. I shall argue that this view is an analytical error, but in part it explains why governments have pursued inconsistent policies, such as simultaneously creating money through QE* [Quantitative Easing – BR] *and trying to reduce government borrowing.*

26   In the original article, my view took the stronger "money is debt" line. I have revised my view to being that the semantic debate is arcane, and one could define terms differently. In any event, the labelling has no operational significance.

27   Eric Lonergan, *Money (Second Revised Edition)*, Routledge, Kindle Edition ISBN: 978-1-84465-823-7.

Although semantic arguments can be fun, they are not useful in the real world. My focus is on finding whether these distinctions make an operational difference in how we analyse the economy. My view is that although it does not really matter where money appears on the government balance sheet, removing it entirely makes analysis extreme awkward.

Firstly, it should be noted that when Lonergan referred to "money" here, it was in reference to the monetary base (that is, "government money"). I am following that convention within this article; this debate has nothing to do with private money, such as bank deposits.

Secondly, this debate is whether money is a liability/debt of the government; money is also an asset on the balance sheet of the entity holding that money. For these non-central government entities, there is no question that it is an asset, it is just about where the corresponding entry is on the central government's balance sheet (or not).

We can now turn to the debate itself.

I will largely skip the debate about money being "debt," although I return to it when I discuss the government debt-to-GDP ratio. The word "debt" has many overtones in common usage, making it difficult to relate to non-technical definitions. When we look at technical definitions of "debt instruments" within securities laws, money probably does not qualify. For a longer argument that money is debt, I would refer the reader to Chapter 8 of *Modern Money Theory* by Randall Wray.[28] The base idea is that "money buys goods and goods buy money, but goods do not buy goods" (quotation originally due to Clower). Since money cannot be a good, Wray's arguments suggest that we end up with it having to be debt. Eric Lonergan's counter-argument is that money does not need to be repaid, and hence cannot be a debt. *(My view is that if we abolish money from economics, then we can skip that whole debate.)*

We now turn to the question of whether money is a liability for the government. It should be noted that under usual national accounting conventions, money is indeed a liability. Eric Lonergan recognises this, but he argues that this is a mistake on the part of the accounting conventions.

On any balance sheet, we place the assets of an entity on the left-hand

---

28   *Modern Money Theory: A Primer on Macroeconomics for Sovereign Monetary Systems*, L. Randall Wray. Palgrave Macmillan, 2012. ISBN: 978-0-230-36889-7.

side, and "Liabilities" and "Equity" on the right.[29] Double-entry accounting ensures that the value of assets equals the value of liabilities plus equity. The way to stop classifying money as a liability is to move it to some category of "equity" (or capital).

Although I have my doubts about such a step, there are precedents. The U.S. Internal Revenue Service (the federal tax agency) reclassified 50-year bonds as a form of equity – since they did not want corporations claiming the interest of such instruments as an expense. Similarly, various fixed income instruments issued by banks are classified as "capital," because of regulatory capture. Therefore, I am open to the idea of reshuffling instruments between being a "liability" and "capital." However, since money holders have no voting rights, and they have a definite nominal claim value, this is not a form of common equity (for example, like the shares of a corporation).

Although I am not particularly concerned where money would appear on the right-hand side of the government's balance sheet, dropping it completely from the government's balance sheet leads to incoherent accounting. One rule of thumb of accounting is that financial operations (such as issuing a bond) will rearrange balance sheet items, but it does not affect common equity. If money were dropped from the government's balance, any financial operation that results in the money outstanding changing would result in the government's equity position changing. If the government issues bonds which are paid for with "money," the government's equity would drop – it would add a new liability item (the auctioned bonds), while the redeemed money would have no effect on the balance sheet (under this accounting convention). Equity would have to fall in order for the balance sheet to balance, which implies some form of expense. Even stranger phenomena would also occur; if a taxpayer paid an outstanding tax bill with money, the government would actually suffer a drop in equity – the taxes payable asset would decrease, while the reduction of money outstanding would have no effect on the balance sheet.

What about the Debt-to-GDP Ratio?

The debate described in the previous section was largely semantic, and did

---

29   In some reporting conventions, the liabilities and equity appear below the assets. This is much less convenient as a teaching tool, as we no longer have two sides of the balance sheet to balance.

not really translate into operational statements about how the economy operates. As a result, we cannot say that Lonergan and Wray are "right" or "wrong" in the sense of being able to compare theoretical predictions to real-world behaviour. However, there do appear to be operational differences if we are worried about modelling government "debt" dynamics.

Let us imagine that we are talking to a junior analyst at a credit rating agency who has to update the spreadsheet that holds the quantitative metrics used to determine the credit rating. One of the variables in the spreadsheet is the "net debt-to-GDP" ratio, so how do we calculate it? (The *gross debt-to-GDP ratio* would be the sum of all of the notional values of all government debt outstanding, while the *net debt-to-GDP ratio* removes from consideration the debt that the government itself has bought back. Such purchases may have been made by the central bank, or by a government-run pension fund.)

A related question is: what happens to the government's net debt when the central bank engages in Quantitative Easing (the purchase of government bonds by the central bank, known as QE)? In this case, the amount of bonds held by the public decreases, while the monetary base (mainly in the form of deposits at the central bank) increases. (Quantitative easing obviously has no effect on gross government debt, but credit ratings should be based on net debt.)

- If the monetary base is not government debt, QE reduces government net debt outstanding.
- If the monetary base is part of governmental debt, then QE has no effect on government net debt; all that happens is that there was a reshuffle of the weightings of that debt (from bonds to "money").

For example, according to the analysis of economist Masazumi Wakatabe of Waseda University, the net debt figures for Japan dropped from 126% of GDP to 41% of GDP in 2014.[30] (Figure 24 shows the IMF annual series for Japanese net debt, which is the source of the 126% number.) Returning to our hypothetical analyst, should he or she include the monetary base in the net debt number of the spreadsheet?

---

30   As quoted in an article by Tom Elliott. "Japanese government bonds: Japan doesn't owe as much as it says it does," *Eurobiz Japan*, February 2016. URL: http://eurobiz.jp/archived-pdfs/EURObiZ_Feb2016.pdf

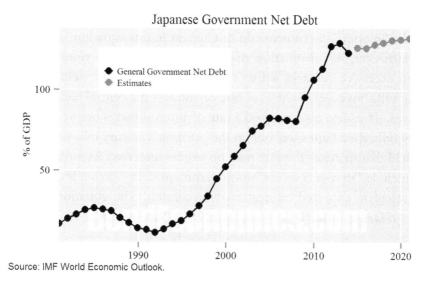

Figure 24. *Japanese net debt-toGDP.*

The correct answer is for the analyst to tell the senior analysts at the rating agency that the probability of an involuntary default by a currency sovereign is 0%, and so it does not matter what figure is used for the net debt-to-GDP ratio in the spreadsheet. However, that would likely be a career-limiting move, and so the analyst has to come up with a less flippant response.

We need to analyse how juggling numbers between the monetary base and government debt (bonds and bills) affects the rest of the economy. We can run simulations of economic trajectories, and see whether the reallocation created by QE affects economic outcomes.

The key difference between "money" and "debt" (bonds and bills) is the interest flow.

- Currency and required reserves generally do not pay interest.
- Bonds and bills pay interest.

We can approximate the expected steady state annual interest cost as (ignoring term premia):

$$(Annual\ Interest\ Cost) = (Expected\ Policy\ Rate) \times (Market\ Value\ of\ Bonds\ and\ Bills).^{31}$$

---

31   Standard market efficiency arguments tell us the expected steady state interest cost for bonds is equal to the market value of the bonds

This creates an obvious difference between bonds and bills ("debt") versus currency and required reserves ("money") within economic models, as the "money" instruments do not appear in this equation.

However, this distinction does not apply to excess reserves. If there is an excess of reserves within the banking system, the yield on Treasury bills will converge to whatever rate of interest the central bank pays on reserves. (If excess reserves paid a rate of interest that is below that of Treasury bills, then banks will bid up the price on Treasury bills until they have a yield that matches the rate paid on excess reserves.) As a result, we need to include "excess reserves" to government debt outstanding if we want to calculate expected interest costs accurately. The equation now reads:

(Annual Interest Cost) = (Expected Policy Rate)×(Market Value of Bonds, Bills, and Excess Reserves).

Since excess reserves also appear in the annual interest cost equation, Quantitative Easing will have no effect on interest costs (ignoring effects such as term premia). We cannot distinguish the effect of excess reserves from government debt within the model, and so excess reserves would needed to be added into governmental net figures for analysis purposes.

Concluding Remarks

Whether or not you consider "money" to be "debt" is pretty much a personal choice, akin to choosing your favourite genre of music. However, one still needs to be careful in how you define "money" if you want to distinguish it from "debt" within economic models – we cannot assume that all components of the monetary base are distinguishable from debt.

---

times the short rate, plus a term premium. In this case, I am assuming that the term premium is zero. If we want to use the notional amount of bonds outstanding in calculations, we would need to take into account the already locked-in yields on the existing stock of bonds.

15 Positive Money

This essay contains some material that was previously published in "Is 100% Reserve Banking Feasible?" (May 13, 2015) and the review of the book The Solution is Full Reserve/100% Reserve Banking, *by Ralph S. Musgrave (July 22, 2015).*

Positive Money is the latest incarnation of an old idea: full reserve banking. There have been a number of proposed schemes over the years, but they all have the same intended effect: taking away banks' ability to "create money." I believe that these proposals mainly reflect unhappiness with bankers from both ends of the political spectrum, as well as an irrelevant fixation on "money." Banking has evolved into its current form for good economic reasons, and we know how to regulate such systems. The failures in recent decades reflect a utopian belief that markets are inherently self-regulating, which tells us more about the failures of economic teaching than banking.

What "Money" Are We Talking About?

One problem with discussing this topic is the multiplicity of proposals that have been made over the decades. One source for more information is the book *The Solution is Full Reserve/100% Reserve Banking*, by Ralph S. Musgrave. (Unfortunately, that book does not offer comprehensive discussions of the original proposals, and the reader is forced to dig further in the primary literature.)

I will instead offer a simplified version, which I believe captures the spirit of various schemes, although not every detail. As I discuss below, this simplified version has obvious flaws when we look at how real-world financial systems operate.

One of the core ideas is that private banks are not supposed to create "money." The first problem is that we need to pin down the definition of "money." We cannot say that banks alone in the private sector create "money" if we use a monetary aggregate like M3, which includes instruments such as repos and money market funds. Instead, we focus on a narrow aggregate.

We cannot use some narrow legalistic definitions as such definitions are very easy to evade.

Instead, we have to use an operational definition for which private sector instruments we consider as "money." The key is access to what I will call herein the "retail payment system" (which is not the same thing as the wholesale interbank payments system, such as Fedwire or Canada's Large Value Transfer system).

Example functions within the retail payment system include:

- Taking in deposits from clients that are covered by deposit insurance.
- Access to the debit card and direct deposit systems.
- Access to automated teller systems.
- Access to cheque (check) clearing systems (although this function is becoming obsolete).

Understanding the Current Situation

Partial Bank Balance Sheet	
Assets	*Liabilities*
$80 Loans	$100 Deposit
$10 Reserves	
$10 Liquid Assets	

Figure 25. *Assets backing deposits.*

Figure 25 gives a simple example of the structure of the current system (assuming a 10% reserve requirement). The client has a $100 deposit at a bank (the deposit is an asset of the client and a liability of the bank). The bank holds assets against that deposit – reserves at the central bank ($10), liquid assets ($10), and loans ($80). (Obviously, these are simplified balance sheets; banks do not match particular assets against particular deposits, and I am ignoring the bank's equity.) Liquid assets for the bank might include Treasury bills, vault cash, excess reserves at the central bank, or liquid bond issues.

As is well publicised by people with an axe to grind against the banking system, this means that liquid deposits are mainly backed by illiquid assets (loans in this case). This creates the possibility of a "bank run," in which people attempt to withdraw deposits, and such a demand could not be met if everyone attempted to withdraw money at once.

Bank runs by depositors were a common event in earlier eras. However, they have largely been eliminated by the application of deposit insurance and central bank lender-of-last-resort facilities. (We still see runs on banks in the wholesale money markets, which sometimes finally result in lines of retail depositors trying to pull out their money. The depositor lineups only tend to occur after the bank has been shut out of the money markets, and the bank is already at death's door.) Although deposit insurance is largely automatic, the application of lender-of-last-resort operations requires the use of judgement by the employees of the central bank: is the borrowing bank merely having a temporary liquidity problem, or is it in a negative equity position (and should be shut down)?

Those guarantees are the target of full reserve banking backers. On the right, they have the strong political belief that the government should not interfere with markets, and all government interventions must be rule-based. In other words, government employees should not be allowed to think. On the left, there is a general animus against bankers, particularly bankers at "too big to fail" banks, and there is a desire for the government to throw said bankers under the bus at every opportunity.

The objection to deposit insurance is somewhat different. Although deposit insurance is more rule-based, there is a belief that it is a subsidised level. Whether or not deposit insurance is subsidised is an open question, and it depends upon which banking system we are analysing. (For example, since no major Canadian bank has failed since the advent of deposit insurance, Canadian deposit insurance appears to have been overpriced.) Since bank failures reflect economic structure and the business cycle, they cannot be the subject of actuarial analysis similar to that used in the insurance industry (for example, fire insurance). Setting the premiums for deposit insurance is always going to be a judgement call by national regulators. Furthermore, if deposit insurance is needed, it reflects a failure by the authorities to regulate the banking system properly. That regulatory failure is the problem, not the deposit insurance.

Means of Eliminating Risk From Deposits

It is relatively straightforward to eliminate the risks associated with a bank defaulting on its deposits. All of the remedies rely on requiring 100% backing by Treasury bills (and bonds), with differing modes of financial intermediation between depositors and Treasury bills. Such schemes already exist, but they are economically unsatisfactory. The side effect of these schemes is that bank loans would no longer be funded with deposits, which will break financial intermediation. I discuss that side effect later. There are three main plausible means of eliminating deposit risk.[32]

1. Banks are forced to hold reserves in an amount equal to "demand deposits." These reserves are deposits at the central bank, and the balance sheets of developed countries' central banks almost entirely consist of Treasury bills and bonds. (Central banks have some residual gold holdings and possibly foreign exchange reserves, but those assets are smaller than currency in circulation. Therefore, Treasury holdings would be larger than reserves.)

2. Private sector Treasury bill mutual funds would have access to the "retail payments" system.

3. The central government could (re-)create postal banking systems: citizens do their deposit banking at branches located at post offices. The postal banking system would hold Treasury bills/bonds in a trust fund against those deposits. (Whether or not those holdings would be netted out of the consolidated government sector is mainly the result of whims of national accountants. From an economic point of view, those deposits are just a new form of direct liability of the Treasury.) The postal bank would not offer any lending services, other than the possible exception of overdraft protection (which can be viewed as a loan).

Importantly, all three sensible modes of intermediation could coexist; they just need to use a common retail payments system.

Interestingly enough, such deposit intermediation could be offered now, with almost no major changes to regulation. However, such schemes would be highly uneconomical – as discussed in the following section. That said, I believe that there is a public purpose argument for reviving postal banking, in at least some countries.[33] The political problem is no

---

32   There is an implausible method: allow everyone to set up an account at the central bank. Central banks generally lack the capacity to bring in a large number of clients. The Bank of England used to offer banking services to its employees, but is now winding those operations up.

33   In particular, postal banking in my home country of Canada

doubt that such a system would end up being subsidised, which would make it a target for right-wing politicians. Although some libertarians object to government meddling in banking with fractional reserve lending, they dislike government subsidies even more.

The Lousy Economics of Full Reserve Banking

My main objections to full reserve banking involve the problems with the effect on bank lending, but even the provision of safe deposits is unattractive. As I discuss in this section, the provision of fully reserved deposits that have access to the "retail payments system" is unlikely to be economic.

If we ignore most of the other activities of banks, the pre-tax profits associated with deposit-taking are as follows:

(Net profits) = *(Treasury bill yield times deposit amount)* + *(profits due to credit spread)* - *(interest paid on deposits)* – *(cost of retail banking)* – *(deposit insurance premiums)*.

The equation decomposes the return from bank lending into two components: the return from investing in Treasury bills, and the credit spread earned from riskier lending.

Although banks are generally profitable entities, their profits are only large relative to their equity base – not the total size of their asset holdings. The implication is that total profits cannot be greatly reduced. If we assume that profits are unchanged, the implication is that the effective interest rate paid on deposits would have to be reduced by the amount of the credit spread on bank lending. Since that interest rate is already zero for many deposit accounts, deposit taking institutions would be forced to levy high fixed fees to make up for the lost interest income. (Charging a negative interest rate implies that the institution would be charging its biggest clients the biggest fees, which would easily be a commercial disaster.)

---

seems pointless. With only a small number of banks dominating the banking sector, regulators can easily force the banks to provide minimal services to the poor who would otherwise be "unbanked." Since the major banks would be roughly equally burdened, this would not cause major competitive distortions. Regulators could strong-arm banks into providing those services by finding employees who say things like "That's a nice a banking license you have there, it would be a shame if something happened to it."

From the perspective of most depositors, such a change is quite negative. Bank fees would greatly increase, while there would be no change in the riskiness of the deposits – since the majority of people's deposits are below the deposit insurance limit.

Furthermore, it is unclear why any institutions would want to offer deposit services in the first place. For banks in the current framework, deposits are a reliable low cost source of funding, and so they have an incentive to build out a branch system. Since banks generally lend to their own depositors, they also have an incentive to offer services to the people who have to pay back the bank's loans – even if the amount they have on deposit is small. In a full reserve system, deposit taking is almost purely a question of technology and customer service, and the winners are those with the minimum servicing costs. In the current environment, it is safe to predict that it would be dominated by a few big players that would have little interest in keeping their smaller customers.

In summary, creating a perfectly safe deposit system can be done, even without major changes to the current institutional framework. The problem is that the system would end up being highly costly for most depositors, without any tangible benefits for individuals. The more negative effects of the proposals involve the lending activities of banks, which is the next topic of discussion.

Destroying the Banking System – Not a Bright Idea

In order to fulfil their dreams, the "full reserve banking" proponents need to destroy the free market in the credit system (although the supporters from the University of Chicago might want to use a different phrasing). In order to implement these proposals, financing forms would have to be rigidly regulated. Otherwise, financial innovations would most likely end up replicating the logic of fractional reserve lending.

The various full reserve proposals provide different methods for credit financing, but the methods generally resemble the functioning of retail fixed income mutual funds (unit trusts) work. These funds expose the investors (unit holders) to risk, and may have restrictions upon withdrawal. (Since loans cannot be paid on demand, the idea is that a fund cannot be expected to redeem units on demand, unlike a bank deposit.)

One example is given proposals by *PositiveMoney.org*, a group in the

United Kingdom calling for full reserve banking (which they call "positive money"), in the document "Creating a Sovereign Monetary System."[34] In their proposal, two types of accounts are to be created; one a fully-backed transaction account as described earlier, and the second an investment account. These accounts are described as follows:

After the reform banks would provide two distinct types of account to businesses and members of the public: Transaction Accounts and Investment Accounts. An overview of these two accounts is given now, and further detail below.

The payments services would be based on Transaction Accounts held by businesses and members of the public. The funds in these accounts would not be deposits created by the banks (an IOU from the bank to a customer), but electronic sovereign money, originally created by the central bank. ...

... [Rest of description deleted; this is similar to the systems described earlier. – BR]

The intermediary function of banks would take place through Investment Accounts. A customer wishing to make savings or investments in order to earn interest would transfer funds from their Transaction Account into an Investment Pool owned by the bank. The bank would set up an Investment Account for the customer, which is a liability of the bank representing the investment made (and the bank's obligation to repay the funds in the future). The customer would have to agree to either a notice period required before accessing his/her money, or a maturity date on which the investment will be repaid. There would be no 'instant-access' investment accounts.

Unfortunately, many of the backers of these proposals – particularly free market-oriented academics – assume that all markets behave like equity markets. The underlying assumption is that *all* financial assets have a well-defined price, and so that we mark them to market on a regular basis. *The credit markets do not work that way.*

Yes, one may point to the relatively liquid markets in investment grade corporate bonds in the developed countries as being a credit market where we do have something resembling a daily mark-to-market. (However, this was not the case during the Financial Crisis.)

For example, imagine that you work for an institutional fixed income

---

34   "Creating a Sovereign Monetary System," by Ben Dyson, Andrew Jackson, Graham Hodgson, *Positive Money*, updated on July 15, 2014. URL: http://positivemoney.org/our-proposals/

investor, which has a monthly mark-to-market procedure. One day, some-one calls you up to get a bid on a $1,000 loan to the owner of *Paul's Pou-tine Palace*. Importantly, this is not a $1,000 piece of a larger loan; that is the total borrowing by the owner (who needed to finance a shipment of potatoes). What is your bid? *The correct bid for such a loan is $0.* The fixed cost of adding a new debt issuer (*Paul's Poutine Palace*) to your systems, and doing the monthly mark-to-market is greater than $1,000. That is, investors within a mark-to-market framework cannot make small loans.

Banks are only able to extend loans to small businesses because they do not mark their loan books to market. They apply loan loss reserves against their books, which are only a statistical measure. Banks concentrate their anal-ysis of most loans to short periods of time – when the loans are first made, and when the loans are no longer current (and they need to mitigate losses).

Whether or not withdrawals are restricted does not help the burden of mark-to-market accounting. If the bank issues units in an investment ac-count based on the Net Asset Value of the investment fund, it has to do a mark-to-market exercise when the money is coming in, as well as when it leaves. (Otherwise, we cannot determine how many units a deposit is worth.)

The only way of avoiding mark-to-market accounting is to structure the deposit as a loan. A lending institution would originate a pool of loans, and then that pool by borrowing money from "depositors." The "depositors" would be paid back as the original loans are themselves paid off, and credit losses would be passed on to the "depositors." Since payments are based only on cash flows from the loan pool, there is no need to find a market value for the loans. Such a structure is essentially a securitisation.

Securitisations do supply small loans. Unfortunately, as was discovered in the Financial Crisis, securitisations are inherently dysfunctional financ-ing structure. To what extent securitisations "work," they need to securitise loans that banks view as acceptable if they were to keep the loans on their own balance sheets (instead of dumping them on securitisation investors). Lending institutions that have no incentive to analyse borrowers' capacity to repay their loans is just going to recreate the failures of the pre-Finan-cial Crisis era.

Such proposals would create a credit system that could only offer fi-nance to large corporations – like most the current shadow banking system. Small businesses and individuals would only be able to borrow based on the access to rich individuals (or mob loan sharks). This would probably create a financial system that even ancient Greeks and Romans might view as primitive.

Control of the Money Supply – A Red Herring

By eliminating "bank money," the full reserve banking proposals appear to fulfil the dream of Monetarists – total control of the "money supply" by the central bank. (This is the source of the phrase "sovereign money.")

The previously cited report by Positive Money argues:

Sovereign money as a solution: Money creation by the central bank would be countercyclical. In times when the economy is booming, rates of money creation would be reduced, to avoid fuelling inflation. But when the economy is in recession, rates of money creation will be increased to prevent prices from falling, leading to additional spending and boosting the economy. This is likely to lead to a much more stable economy.

Such a viewpoint makes little sense, as it relies upon naïve notions about "money," which are inherited from economic theory.

The correct way of looking at this issue is that *credit creation is pro-cyclical.* Credit creation will still exist, even within the institutional framework proposed by full reserve banking proponents.

Anyone who is familiar with evolution of Monetarism notes that the "money supply" figures tracked moved towards wider aggregates over time. Those wider aggregates include money market instruments that are outside the formal banking system. For a fixed income investor, all of these instruments are lumped into the asset class called "cash," and are viewed as largely interchangeable. Some are preferred to others; such instruments just trade at tighter spreads.

There will be short-term investment funds that will be treated as "cash" by private sector entities in the economy. It will be possible to expand balance sheets solely by some entities issuing such short-term securities, and then holding the proceeds in similar short-term securities. For example, a corporation could issue commercial paper, and invest the proceeds in a money market fund – which invests in commercial paper. The commercial paper issuance is self-financing, since money market fund assets will increase by the same amount as the issuance.

(There is a technical niggle – the issuance would require the use of "money" for settlements. However, this is purely an intra-day concern; the net settlements would be zero, and so the "money supply" would be unchanged at the end of the day. Therefore, there is no relationship between the "money supply" – which is what the central bank can control – and credit expansion.)

In summary, the central bank will have no more control over credit expansion than it does in the current framework.

The Elimination of Credit Lines Makes Non-Bank Finance Difficult

One obvious point of failure of these proposals is that they only look at "lending," and ignore credit lines – which are extremely important. There is no economic way of offering credit lines, and at the same time respecting the objectives of the full reserve framework.

If an entity is going to offer a credit line, and it does not itself have an emergency credit line with the central bank (which is what lender-of-last-resort operations are), it either is going to have to gamble on remaining liquid, or match the amount of credit lines it has extended with investments in "money."

As an example of "gambling" with credit lines, a firm could extend $10 million in credit lines, while only having $1 million in "money," while having $9 million invested in various bonds. It essentially has reserves of 10%, and has to hope that it can sell bonds to meet the demands of its clients when they draw on their lines.

Such a firm has essentially become a bank, and in the absence of a central bank, is susceptible to runs. Therefore, such activity would have to be made illegal to be consistent with the rest of the reforms.

Assuming that regulators prevent such activity, the only way to extend a credit line is to back it fully with "money." However, that has disastrous economics for a firm issuing such lines. It is investing in "money," which will have a yield resembling that of Treasury bills (at most), yet its balance sheet is completely illiquid. A completely illiquid balance sheet needs to be funded with equity or long-term debt.

The firm's return on assets will be the Treasury bill yield, plus the fees for credit lines. Its cost of financing would be a mix of long-term bond yields or the equity rate of return. The only way such an activity is going to break even is if the fees on credit lines are extremely high.

Without credit lines, non-bank finance (such as commercial paper issuance programmes) breaks down. Lending on a short-term basis to firms that do not have a credit line is foolhardy; such lines are required in order to get an investment grade rating. Institutional investors in the non-bank financing sector do not have special privileges for obtaining financial information of borrowers, unlike banks. They are forced to rely on the judgement of banks – as evidenced by the extension of credit line – for judging the short-term liquidity position of borrowers.

In summary, full reserve banking proponents want to replace the banking sector with non-bank financing ("shadow banking") without analysing how non-bank financing critically relies upon formal banks.

We Know How to Have a Safe Financial System

If the objective is to have a safe financial system, we know how to get there: take a time machine back to the 1950s. Financing was based on fractional reserve bank lending, while the "shadow banking" system was rudimentary. Government financing dominated the bond market, and corporate issuers tenaciously held on to their AAA ratings. Meanwhile, bank balance sheets were stuffed with Treasury bills, because of high debt-to-GDP ratios that were the result of World War II. The reality is that it is very difficult for a run on a bank to develop if most of its balance sheet consists of Treasury bill allocations that are *voluntarily held*.

(One of the big ideas floating around in regulatory circles currently is *forcing* banks to hold a certain percentage of their balance sheets as liquid assets. This is pointless financial repression. If liquid assets cannot be liquidated as doing so would drive the bank below its regulatory limit, those holdings do not actually help the liquidity position of the bank. In order to be liquid, a bank must hold liquid assets beyond any regulatory minimum.)

Although bank-driven financing was a feature of most developed countries in the early post-war period, it is also a feature of the industrialised countries that graduated to rich country status. The Japanese, German, and South Korean economies featured industrial groups that were built around domestic bank financing. I do not have any expertise in development economics, but I cannot think of a single country that actually developed a strong economy using non-bank finance (without relying on dodges like oil wealth or being a tax haven).

Many of the full reserve banking proponents are strong believers in free markets, and project their belief that all business activity should be organised as transparent auctions (like futures or equity markets). As a result, they want credit financing to be organised in markets – that is, shadow banking – instead of opaque bank lending. However, that is moving in exactly the wrong direction from the stable bank-driven lending of the 1950s.

That said, it would not be easy to roll back the clock. Hyman Minsky's career as an economist chronicled the evolution of the financial system from stable bank-driven institutions to the market-driven crisis-prone institutions of the present (an evolution that he predicted). The stability of the early post-war era was driven by the fear of the Great Depression, which took the animal spirits out of the financial markets. However, market participants and banks chafed under the restrictive regulations, and continuously created "financial innovations," which were just means to bypass regulations. When those market-based financing arrangements blew up in a crisis, governments stepped in and bailed out the system, ratifying the "innovations."

Absent a similar political crisis that once again forces people to take the stability of capitalism seriously, once again, I do not see magic bullets to solve financial instability. Institutional structures in the developed world have created large pools of capital outside of the banking system (for example, pension funds). That capital is invariably going to be deployed in foolish pro-cyclical ways in the shadow banking system.

The best we can hope for is to stamp out the obviously idiotic forms of financing that pop up, and keep the playing field roughly level between the regulated banks and unregulated "shadow banks." Slapping pointless reserve requirements on banks hastens the demise of the regulated system at the hands of unregulated finance, and so it is a step to be avoided.

Concluding Remarks

It is very easy to be angry with the financiers who wreaked havoc in the lead-up to the Financial Crisis. However, we should not pick on the easy targets – banks who are already regulated – and skip over the real source of financial instability, the non-bank financial system.

16 Central Banks as Pawnbrokers

The original version of this essay was published on November 13, 2016.

Lord Mervyn King (Governor of the Bank of England from 2003 to 2013) wrote *The End of Alchemy: Money, Banking, and the Future of the Global Economy.*[35] In it, he discusses a banking reform, in which the central bank becomes a "pawnbroker for all seasons" (Chapter 7). The proposal is very similar to one I discussed in *Understanding Government Finance* – which was proposed by Hyman Minsky, which in turn was based on central bank operating procedures from before World War II. I agree with Lord King about the proposal, however, my interpretation of how it should be implemented differs. At the root of the issue is my feeling that his worldview shares too many assumptions taken from Monetarism.

A Pawnbroker for All Seasons?

One of the advantages of the proposal is that it greatly simplifies bank regulation. Almost all of the existing banking regulatory scheme could be thrown in the dumpster, and replaced by two basic principles (please note that this is my rephrasing of the book's description):

1. *All* financial entities that issue short-term financial liabilities (including bank deposits, in case that is not obvious) must ensure that their *effective liquid assets* are at least the same size as their short-term liabilities (he uses one-year maturity as a cut-off). *(In this text, I use "bank" for simplicity, but it must be emphasised that non-bank financial entities are caught up in this regulatory web as well.)*

2. *Effective liquid assets* are defined as the sum of the value of a firm's assets after taking into account a liquidity haircut that is defined by the central bank (based on the class of assets). This is discussed further below.

The haircut can be between 0% and 100%. An asset that is fully liq-

---

35   *The End of Alchemy: Money, Banking and the Future of the Global Economy,* Mervyn King, W.M. Norton & Company, 2016. ISBN: 978-0-393-24702-2.

uid – for example, a deposit at the central bank – has a 0% haircut. This means that the entire holding amount counts towards the effective liquid asset total. Conversely, some toxic piece of financial engineering (such as a CDO-squared) would get a haircut of 100%, and would not count at all towards effective liquid assets.

For example, take the classic case of a bank with assets that consist of $10 in balances at the central bank, and $90 in bank loans. If the loans all fell into a category for which the haircut was 50%, the effective liquid asset total of the bank is calculated as $55 ($10 for the reserves, and $45 for the bank loans). The implication is that the bank cannot have more than $55 in short-term liabilities; the remaining $45 would have to consist of long-dated bonds and equity.

In practice, a bank would need to operate with excess effective liquidity. This would probably take the form of holding short-term government securities (or deposits at the central bank) which would have a haircut around 0%. For example, if a bank extends a $100 loan, and the haircut on the loan is 50%, it would need $50 of excess effective liquidity. In this example, this is achieved by holding $50 on deposit at the central bank (beyond what is needed to cover the regulatory minimum). If that borrower transfers the $100 to another bank, the lending bank will be able to cover the withdrawal as follows:

1. it would transfer $50 in excess reserves to the other bank; and
2. it would borrow $50 from the central bank, using the loan as collateral.

(The only other part of bank regulation that would also be needed is the regulation of the breakdown between long-term debt and equity. In theory, it should not matter too much, since if the institution falls to a negative equity position, regulators have a year to do a debt restructuring. In practice, regulators are not going to want to have large universal banks holding the economy hostage by threatening to go bust at a bad time.)

Importantly, the "haircuts" are not just a regulatory concept, like asset risk weightings in current regimes; they have an operational importance. The central bank is committed to lend against those assets on demand, with the amount of the loan set by the largely fixed haircut schedule. (The central bank may revise those haircuts, but only at infrequent intervals, such as three years.) The interest rate on such loans would be at a fixed spread to the policy rate of interest.

Full reserve banking (100% bank reserves) can be viewed as a special case of this scheme. In full reserve banking, the haircut on all assets other than settlement balances at the central bank and Treasury bills is 100%.

Difference from Bagehot's "Lender of Last Resort"

Central bank lending against collateral can be viewed as a form of lender-of-last-resort operation. However, King observes that there is a difference from Walter Bagehot's formulation: the central bank should lend freely against *good* collateral in a crisis.

Unfortunately, what we see in practice is that banks "optimise" their balance sheets during the expansion phase of the cycle, and they keep the regulatory minimum amount of unambiguously "good" collateral. When the crisis hits, all that banks are stuck with is "bad" collateral.

By pre-committing to lend against specific classes of assets at fixed haircuts, the central bank is going to lend against *almost any* collateral in a crisis (although it would likely rule out in advance fixed income securities it cannot price, or equity securities, by setting the haircut at 100%).[36]

Back to the Future

I have advocated a similar scheme, so I certainly agree with the basic principles behind Lord King's suggestion. However, I have some reservations about the implementation – I believe that central banks need to embrace this concept even more forcefully. Instead of just being an operation undertaken during a crisis, central bank lending against private sector collateral should be done on a full-time basis.

---

36   I have some reservations with this argument. I interpret Bagehot's definition of "good collateral" as "good under normal circumstances, but perhaps not during a crisis." For example, BBB-rated industrial bonds are normally "good collateral," but might not be viewed as such in the middle of a crisis. I would not view lending against such securities as "lending against bad collateral." The Financial Crisis was unusual in that the financial system managed to convince itself that some extremely toxic financial structures were "money good," but one hopes that investors will not be that gullible again for a long time. It makes no sense to ever lend against truly "bad" collateral, such as debt of firms in the middle of a restructuring.

My analysis is not particularly original; my arguments were based on Hyman Minsky's; for example, he discusses this in Chapter 13 of *Stabilizing an Unstable Economy*.[37] (My summary was published in Chapter A.2 of *Understanding Government Finance*.) Meanwhile, his comments were based on returning central bank operations to how they were undertaken in earlier eras, such as by the Bank of England before World War I.[38]

In Minsky's version of the policy, the central bank's balance sheet will consist almost entirely of discounted private sector assets at all times (and not just during crises). Such a policy stance is sometimes referred to as an "overdraft economy," and is discussed in Marc Lavoie's *Post-Keynesian Economics: New Foundations*.[39] By necessity, banks (and selected "shadow bank" institutions) would have to go to the central bank for short-term financing. Central bank staff would be forced to follow closely the trends in assets held by the banking system. If the central bank does not like the risk profile taken by banks, it eliminates the short-term financing for the dodgy lending, forcing the banks to either use long-term financing to fund the loans, or stop making such types of loans.

The central bank will thus always be forced to keep an eye on what the bankers are up to, and nudge the private sector towards less self-destructive paths. We would not repeat the experience of the Financial Crisis, where central bankers suddenly woke up to the reality that they had no idea what private financiers had been up to over the past decade.

One additional point to keep in mind that the discounted collateral is only the second line of defence for central bank lending – the original bank still owes the money to the central bank, regardless of the value of the collateral. Therefore, the central bank is not completely exposed to the risk of private sector entities creating toxic securities that are dumped on the central bank at no risk to the private sector firms. Of course, the

37   *Stabilizing an Unstable Economy*, Hyman P. Minsky, McGraw-Hill, 2008. ISBN: 978-0-07-159299-4.

38   Minsky cites R.S. Sayers, *Bank of England Operations (1890-1914)*, (London: P.S. King And Sons, 1936), a volume to which I do not have access.

39   Found on pages 208-209 of *Post-Keynesian Economics: New Foundations*, Marc Lavoie, Edward Elgar Publishing Limited, 2014. ISBN 978-1-78347-582-7.

central bank will need to ensure that the private firms have sufficient equity to back up their discount window borrowings, which means that the central bank still must understand the capital structure of its counterparties. This means that under these proposals, the central bank has to look at the entirety of regulated firms' balance sheets, and not just focus on the collateral. (The responsibility for the payments system means that the central bank has to have a good grasp of financial sector solvency anyway.)

Of course, there will still be ugly shocks. The reality is that lending standards will always be pro-cyclical; the shifts in "animal spirits" almost entirely defines the business cycle (other than the case of boneheaded policy-induced recessions, such as the present situation in the euro area periphery). Central bankers are human, and so they will be sucked into the latest investment fads as well. However, their institutions cannot go bust, and so they will be in a good position to work things out. As long as the private banks survive the crisis, the central bank will not be exposed.

It would have been interesting to see how Mervyn King compares his proposal to the analysis of Minsky. In fact, Mervyn King cites *Stabilizing an Unstable Economy* in the *End of Alchemy*, so it is not as if he was completely unaware of Minsky's work (!). My guess is that King only looked at the parts of Minsky's book that discussed the "Financial Instability Hypothesis," and ignored the sections on how Minsky wanted to reform capitalism to stabilise an unstable economy.

Monetarism, Again

Although Mervyn King does not appear to be a Monetarist, he has incorporated a hidden analytical assumption that mainstream economics picked up from Monetarism. *(My comments here are based on Minsky's observations about Monetarism.)* Historically, central bankers were, well, bankers. However, Monetarists were fixated on the magical variable *"M"* in economic models, and insisted that the only role of the central bank was to set the level of "the money supply" in some optimal fashion. Ideally, *all* discretion would be removed from central bank activity; everything would be rule-based. (Professor John Taylor's arguments about rule-based policy rates are just a variant of this view.)

If the central bank just buys Treasury securities, there is almost no discretion in its decision-making. (The trading desk has limited discretion, but they normally just act to keep bond prices in line with a fitted yield curve, similar to what private sector relative value strategists do.) Deciding what loans to discount, and what haircuts to apply, brings back discretion in a big way.

As a Canadian Prairie Populist (who admittedly lives about 2000 kilometres from the nearest prairie), I understand the political problems with central bankers cutting opaque deals with fat cat bankers. Nevertheless, that is how private sector finance largely works. Banks routinely have to decide which borrowers will have their loans rolled over, and which will end up being restructured (if the borrower cannot find an alternative source of financing). There are markets that are transparent – such as equity secondary market trading, and the futures market – but those markets are used for shuffling existing portfolios, not for raising capital.

Absent a total restructuring of the financial system, it is extremely difficult to prohibit central bank staff from making relatively opaque decisions with respect to lender-of-last resort operations. What could be done, for example, big banks could be broken up, to avoid "too big to fail" issues (and reduce the lobbying power of individual bank lobbyists). Nevertheless, the Savings and Loan crisis in the United States demonstrated that a group of small banks can all run over the same cliff in the same manner as big banks, and that even relatively small banks can manage to develop strong political connections. (This episode is discussed in Bill Black's book, *The Best Way to Rob a Bank Is to Own One.*[40] In the book, Black describes his experiences as regulator during that crisis.) At the end of the day, we have to rely on the professional integrity of central bank staff, and not hope that disembodied "policy rules" can magically make all economic problems disappear.

---

40   *The Best Way to Rob a Bank Is to Own One: How Corporate Executives and Politicians Looted the S&L Industry,* William K. Black, University of Texas Press, 2005. ISBN: 0-292-72139-0

17 Coming to Grips with "Helicopter Money"

This essay has not been previously published in this form, but is partly based on earlier articles.

The idea of "helicopter money" has come up repeatedly since the Financial Crisis, and with policy rates very close to zero, it is one of the few options that monetary policy-obsessed economists can come up with to deal with the next downturn. Unfortunately, it is very unclear how these policies are supposed to work. This essay discusses various forms of "helicopter money," and the related idea of "overt monetary financing."

I prefer the use of "helicopter money," as I have seen two very distinct meanings attached to "overt monetary financing." Although the two meanings look similar, they are miles apart in terms of policy implementation.

Origins of "Helicopter Money"

The origins of the phrase can be traced to Milton Friedman. He wished to discuss economies in easy-to-understand terms, and he needed to explain how central banks control the "money supply." That is, he wanted to illustrate how "exogenous money" worked in the real world. In his example, he imagined central bankers hopping into helicopters, and dropping money onto the citizenry.

This sounds crazy, but that just reflects the fact that central bankers do not actually control the money supply. (I discuss this further in "Primer: Endogenous Versus Exogenous Money" – Section 10.) If you need a nonsensical story to explain how your theoretical framework operates, that is a good reflection on the weakness of your framework.

This usage of the term "helicopter money" is a digression, but it is covered here, as one occasionally runs into writers who discuss what Milton Friedman *really meant.*

An Operational Perspective on Governmental Liabilities

One of the difficulties with helicopter money is that there are multiple proposed implementations, and those implementations only have vague descriptions. We need to look back, take a simplified view of (central) governmental finance, and see how helicopter money proposals fit into that viewpoint.

One of the key analytical assumptions I am making here is that I am consolidating the central bank with the rest of the government (in particular, the financing arm, or Treasury). I discuss consolidation in more detail in Section 3.5 of *Understanding Government Finance*. Although it is a fancy-sounding word, it just means to lump the finances of the central bank with the rest of the government. From the perspective of anyone outside the central government, there is generally no distinction between the central bank and the Treasury. The exception is concerning the possibility of default. Finally, consolidation is not applicable for the euro area, as the European Central Bank is not under the control of anything else. As a result, my comments here are not fully applicable to the euro area, and so "helicopter money" may make more sense within that institutional framework.

The central government issues five categories of liabilities[41] as part of its financial operations.

1. currency (notes and coins);
2. required reserves at the central bank;
3. excess reserves (settlement balances) at the central bank;
4. Treasury bills; and
5. government bonds.

The first three categories of liabilities essentially comprise the "monetary base," and so are "money" to most people. However, they have completely different behavioural properties when it comes to the financing costs associated with them.

Famously, the first category of liabilities – currency – does not normally pay interest. This property is what creates the so-called "zero lower bound" for interest rates. (It is possible to have "stamped money" which can have an interest rate associated with it – positive or negative – but such schemes are unpopular.) It should be noted that some economists are calling for the replacement of currency with electronic money – to allow

---

41   As I discuss in "Money as Debt," there are arguments that some forms of money (such as currency) are not "liabilities." Although an interesting linguistic discussion, I defer to national accounting standards here, in which all of these categories are liabilities.

negative interest rates. (I discuss this further in "Abolishing Currency in the Real World is Just Plain Nuts," Section 21).

The second category of liabilities is required reserves held at the central bank. Banking regulations in some countries (notably the United States) require banks to hold these reserves. In other countries, such as Canada, these reserve requirements do not exist. The amount of reserves a bank is required to hold is normally calculated based on the amount of its deposit liabilities, although not all types of deposits count. Since these required reserves are a regulatory requirement, the central bank can pay whatever rate of interest it wishes upon them. Historically, the rate of interest on required reserves in the United States was 0%, and so they paid the same rate of interest as currency. This somewhat justifies blurring the distinction between the two categories; one can think of currency as a reserve liability in bearer form.[42]

All of the remaining categories of governmental liabilities pay interest – although that rate of interest could be zero or even "slightly" negative. The interest rates on Treasury bonds and bills are now currently set in auction, although that is purely a convention that people now assume is "natural." The yields on those instruments could be fixed, and the Treasury could instead just issue enough securities to meet demand. (That is, instead of setting the quantity and letting the market determine the price, the government could set the price, and let the market determine the quantity. Since the central government is the monopoly supplier of Treasury securities, it can act like any other monopolist that faces the decision of how to ration its product.)

The exception appears to be excess reserves (settlement balances at the central bank in excess of required reserves). Since they are a deposit at the central bank, their interest rate is purely an administrative decision of the bank. Historically, the Federal Reserve did not pay interest on excess reserves. However, a private bank is not going to leave excess reserves at the central bank returning 0%, if it can instead purchase short-term assets with a higher yield. As a result, unless excess reserves are very small relative to banking system assets (which they historically were; please see the figure

---

42   There may be a distinction as currency may be issued by the Treasury, and not the central bank. That distinction disappears once we consolidate the central bank with the Treasury.

in Section 10), the rate of interest on Treasury bills will converge towards the rate of interest paid on excess reserves. Which means that if there are large excess reserves, and the rate of interest paid on reserves is 0%, the Treasury bill yield will converge towards 0% as well. This is exactly what happened in the post-crisis United States, although the rates of interest involved were actually slightly positive. (The Fed paid 0.25% on excess reserves.)

From the perspective of economic modelling, we cannot be concerned about small deviations between interest rates (approximately 0.25% or less). Even if the government liability-to-GDP ratio hits 100%, a 25 basis point financing gap still represents a difference in interest costs that is 0.25% of GDP. We have no hope of modelling the impact of such a difference upon the economy.

One should note that the expected interest costs on Treasury bonds differ from those of Treasury bills. The standard argument is that bond yields incorporate a risk premium, and so the expected interest cost of issuing a 10-year bond is higher than rolling Treasury bills for 10 years.[43] Although this argument is reasonable, we should still expect the long-term financing cost of bond issuance to be similar to that for bills once we take into account the margins of error in our interest forecasts.

In summary, only required reserves and currency exhibit the 0% interest property that "money" allegedly has.

Types of Helicopter Money

We are now in a position to describe various proposals for helicopter money (and/or overt monetary financing of fiscal policy).

Money literally dropped from helicopters. The central bank distributes money in some random fashion to members of the population. This was the original Milton Friedman idea, but it is not something we are likely to see in the real world. Even if this were tried, the currency dropped from helicopters would almost immediately be returned to the banking system, and we would end up with a policy that looks similar to the other cases listed below. There is no way for the central bank

---

43   Some term structure models currently generate a negative term premium. However, I have my doubts about the usefulness of such models.

to force people to hold currency, with its magical 0% rate of interest.

Central bank-driven transfer payments. The central bank somehow creates a bureaucracy that administers some form of transfer payments to the population. Although theoretically possible in highly abstract models, creating a bureaucracy from scratch to handle an eventuality (hitting the zero lower bound for interest rates) that might occur only once per decade (at most) makes this possibility unrealistic.

The euro area case. The European Central Bank could undertake any number of the possible cases of "helicopter money" discussed here. The policy is much more likely to be effective than is the case for other developed countries, as the central bank is effectively out of the control of the various governments.

The central bank "permanently" creates base money. This is often invoked by mainstream academic economists, and they can often get into intense arcane debates about whether increases in the money supply are "permanent" or not. This only makes sense in a world where base money is exogenous, a possibility that I believe does not apply to the real world (as discussed in "Primer: Endogenous versus Exogenous Money.") Unless the central bank somehow reverts to targeting base money, there is no way we can describe any changes in the money supply as being "permanent."

Changing the Monetary Policy Rule. This is a variation of the previous type, in which the central bank changes how it reacts to economic developments (its "reaction function" in economist jargon). I distinguish it from the previous case, as this provides a coherent explanation of what "permanent" increases in the money supply might mean. (In fact, the money supply could actually end up decreasing in response to economic developments; it is just that the monetary base would be higher than it would have been in the case of an unchanged reaction function. This would not correspond to a common understanding of the word "permanent.") A recent example of this is the Jordi Galí paper – "The Effects of Money-Financed Fiscal Stimulus," which I discuss further in "Money Has Nothing To Do With Overt Monetary Financing" (Section 18). As the title of my essay makes clear, I do not believe that the results have much to do with the role of money (even ignoring the issue of the lack of realism of DSGE models).

Overt Monetary Financing: Central Bank purchases in the pri-

mary market. Many economists and market strategists tend to shudder in horror at the possibility of central banks buying bonds directly from the Treasury. (The *primary market* is where bonds are first issued; currently at auction. Secondary markets are where existing bond holders trade existing holdings amongst themselves, at a market price.) This is often referred to as "monetising deficits," and was a feature of various historical hyperinflations. Although I dismiss this interpretation, it is clear that such policies appear to be necessary condition for a hyperinflation; the problem for this interpretation is that it is not sufficient. For example, the Bank of Canada buys a certain percentage of all Government of Canada bonds that it auctions (acting as an agent for the Ministry of Finance). Meanwhile, Canada has never suffered a hyperinflation.

As long as we are far away from the conditions of a hyperinflation, it will not make a lot of difference whether the central bank buys government bonds in the secondary market or the primary market, as bond yields will reflect the path of the policy rate. This is discussed further in *Understanding Government Finance* (Chapter 6) and *Interest Rate Cycles* (Chapter 4). My argument is that it would be very difficult to construct a model of bond yield determination where it matters whether the central bank is buying bonds at auctions versus in the secondary market; both transactions will have a similar impact on supply and demand positions within the market. The only potential difference is the case where bond auctions fail completely, which I discuss in Section 6.6 of *Understanding Government Finance* (Rollover Risk). As I assert there, we can argue that the risk of a government with a free-floating currency being unable to roll over its debt exists, but this possibility is reliant upon a deliberate mistake by the government (or the desire of the central bank to drive the government into default). Of course, countries that do not control their currency are in a different position, but they are not in a position to undertake "helicopter money" in the first place (with the notable exception of the euro area).

Overt Monetary Financing: Quantitative Easing. In this case, the central bank purchases bonds in the secondary market. (I discussed this in "Primer: Quantitative Easing" – Section 6.) This increases the monetary base, creating excess reserves. As noted earlier, excess reserves pay a rate of interest that is largely indistinguishable from Treasury bills (within minor spread differences). In other words, the net effect on government financing is equivalent to the Treasury replacing bond issuance with bill issuance (and possibly buying back old bonds, and replacing them with bills).

Overt Monetary Financing: Permanent ZIRP. One variation of overt monetary financing is a permanent zero interest rate policy (ZIRP). The government stops issuing bonds, and the short-term policy rate is locked at 0% (or something within a rounding error of 0%, such as 0.25%). The government might issue bills (also at around 0.25%) for private sector entities to use for liquidity management, but it would otherwise rely on "money creation" (mainly excess reserves in the banking system). Some Modern Monetary Theory economists (amongst others) have put this forth as a policy proposal. Whether or not such a policy is a good idea is beyond the scope of this essay.

The key difference from the other variants of "helicopter money" is that in this proposal, the government has reduced the power of the central bank. Conversely, in the other cases, the central bank is given new powers. The government has *permanently* ended the ability of the central bank to set interest rates. All it would do is manage the payments system, undertake lender-of-last-resort operations during financial crises, and regulate banks.

"Financing" spending with increased required reserves. The last class of proposals relies on replacing explicit taxes with an implicit tax: increased required reserves for the banking system. This implicit tax will allow for greater government spending without creating increased demand pressures. As I discuss in "Positive Money" (Section 15), such a proposal is not cost-free: it is a tax on the regulated banking system versus its competitors in the non-bank financial system. In any event, an implicit tax is still a tax, and so it does not really create new space for policy.

Concluding Remarks

A great many policies could be labelled as "Helicopter Money." However, these policies either accomplish nothing, or could be achieved otherwise in a more sensible fashion. The only reason to invoke helicopters is the result of mysticism around money in economics.

18 Money has nothing to do with Overt Monetary Financing

This article was published on October 23, 2016 on BondEconomics.com.

The problem with writing about "Helicopter Money" is that the people advocating it are extremely vague about what it actually is. I looked through the Jordi Galí paper "The Effects of Money-Financed Fiscal Stimulus,"[44] as that paper is heavily cited as providing a formal explanation of how overt monetary financing is supposed to work. Unfortunately, money has nothing to do with the results in that paper.

I will immediately note that some authors use the term "Overt Monetary Financing" for what I consider a completely different policy. Modern Monetary Theory (MMT) authors, particularly Bill Mitchell, and Ralph Musgrave, use "Overt Monetary Financing" to refer to what I would call "permanent ZIRP" (zero interest rate policy). (I discuss this distinction in the previous essay.)

Why Is Fiscal Policy Allegedly Ineffective?

The pre-Financial Crisis consensus was that fiscal policy is ineffective with an independent inflation-targeting central bank: any attempt to stimulate growth by fiscal policy would be cancelled out by the central bank. (There is also the debatable question of Ricardian Equivalence, but that is a second order effect.)

(The mainstream consensus is shifting; but this basic principle is still embedded in most DSGE theory, including the Galí paper.)

Therefore, it is not correct to say that the (original) mainstream position was that fiscal policy was ineffective; it is just that the central bank cancels it out as part of its economic stabilisation mandate.

The "permanent ZIRP" policy would make fiscal policy effective again – because we have shut down the central bank cancellation. (That said,

---

44   Galí, J. 2014. "The Effects of a Money-Financed Fiscal Stimulus." London, Centre for Economic Policy Research. URL: http://www.cepr. org/active/publications/discussion_papers/dp.php?dpno=10165

mainstream economists would be very unhappy at the prospect of the abolition of monetary policy.)

Otherwise, within the mainstream analytical framework, "monetary financing" does not look like it would work: the central bank's inflation-targeting mandate would wipe out the effects of "money-financed" fiscal stimulus. (The zero lower bound cannot be used as a cop-out; at a zero interest rate, Treasury bills are indistinguishable from money.)

Returning to the Galí Paper

The Galí paper has a lot of mathematics in it, which buries what is happening. In my view, the mathematics provides a good distraction from what the paper says.

The results can be summarised: if the central bank no longer cancels out fiscal policy by following a Taylor Rule, fiscal policy is once again effective. If you accept the assumptions of mainstream economics, that is an obvious result. Furthermore, money financing has nothing to do with the conclusions.

The only reason that money appears within the discussion at all is that the paper assumes that there is a stable relationship between "money" and interest rates via a money demand function. Instead of following a rule setting the policy rate – a Taylor Rule – the bank sets the monetary base.

The fact that a mainstream economist is publishing a paper in 2016 which is based upon the concept that "money" is exogenous – an idea which was thoroughly discredited in the 1980s – is rather telling. In the real world, no such stable money demand function exists, and the policy only consists of setting interest rates "too low" in order to generate inflation. "Money financing" only appears in the paper because of the use of this discredited theoretical concept.

DSGE Models Include Finance – Yeah, Right

Apologists for Dynamic Stochastic General Equilibrium (DSGE) models say that the models have improved after the crisis, and include a financial sector. That argument is disproved by the Galí paper: a banking system is nowhere in sight. In reality, the DSGE modelling framework cannot produce realistic results, and all that can be done is that a particular model can attempt to make one particular improvement, but the improvements are not cumulative – other things have to be thrown out to make the model tractable. That is, if a financial sector is added to a model, it has to throw out other things.

We cannot treat the real-world monetary base as the same thing as "money" in a DSGE model that lacks a banking system. The institutional framework around banking is wildly different from currency holdings.

Once again, all of the stochastic calculus embedded in DSGE macro is a distraction from the fact that they provide zero insight into real-world policy decisions.

19 The Political Problems with Helicopter Money

This article previously appeared in draft form on October 9, 2016.

One of the problems with "helicopter money" is that the proponents of the concept give very sketchy and differing descriptions of what it actually is. From my personal perspective, another difficulty with discussing the idea is that I disagree with the politics. Depending on how "helicopter money" is conceived, either it is an insult to the intelligence of the electorate, or it is premised on the idea that politicians are structurally biased towards favouring deflationary policies – a stance for which there is very little evidence.

What is "Helicopter Money"?

I discuss the technical definitions of "helicopter money," in "Coming to Grips with 'Helicopter Money.'" For this essay, I will use two simple definitions that focus on the political economy aspects of the concept.

1. **Overt Monetary Financing.** The central bank "finances" a fiscal stimulus that is controlled by the spending arm of the government (the Treasury or Ministry of Finance).
2. **Central Bank-Directed Stimulus.** The central bank directly implements transfer payments – which is a form of fiscal policy – based on its views of the economic cycle, independent of what the Treasury wishes.

I will discuss these policy options separately, after a digression on the euro area.

The Euro Area Exception

The situation in the euro area is an exception to my discussion here. There is no centralised pan-Euro Treasury of any significant size, and so running significant counter-cyclical fiscal policy might require financing by the European Central Bank.

Many of the proponents of "helicopter money" are European, and are quick to offer the situation in the euro area as an example of the usefulness of helicopter money. Those of us who are non-European have a wider perspective, and realise that we cannot generalise the dysfunctional euro area institutions to other regions.

Finally, I will note my cynicism even concerning the euro area. The European Central Bank was part of "the Troika" which levelled the economies of the European periphery. The ECB is politically unaccountable, and part of the problem of euro area governance. Giving an out-of-control, unaccountable organisation with a horrific decision-making track record more power on the theory that the next episode will turn out better seems questionable.

Overt Monetary Financing

Overt Monetary Financing is a piece of jargon that just says that the central bank will finance Treasury spending. The alleged advantage is that this lowers the probability of Treasury default to 0%, and so the Treasury can spend without worrying about "fiscal sustainability."

Unfortunately, as I discussed in *Understanding Government Finance*, the probability of involuntary default was 0% to begin with.[45] There is no advantage to "Overt Monetary Financing" versus "Standard Government Finance."

The rejoinder is that the electorate is allegedly stupid, and they do not understand that governments with currency sovereignty cannot be forced to involuntarily default. My response is that the people backing "helicopter money" are implicitly peddling myths about "financial constraints," and are part of the problem, and not part of the solution.

In any event, the issue is that the Treasury has to want to undertake the extra spending that is "financed with money." Since politicians appear to understand government finance better than many economists do, they are likely to be skeptical about such schemes. Instead, they will only spend what they wanted to spend in the first place, and they know that they can achieve such spending using standard government financing techniques.

This leads into the next section, where the central bank takes control of spending.

---

45   Yes, there are some obvious disclaimers to that categorical statement. For example, a government that disappears in a war is unlikely to meet the principal payments on its bonds. **Understanding Government Finance** discusses the details at greater length. I would like to thank the commenter "Barney Rubbles" on the website **Seeking Alpha** for noting that the phrasing in an earlier draft was too broad.

Central Bank-Led Fiscal Policy

The central bank can lead the horse to water, but cannot force it to drink. Therefore, there are arguments that the central bank should engage in fiscal policy: transferring money to citizens as part of economic stabilisation policy.

The economic justification is the dreaded "zero lower bound": with the policy rate stuck at 0%, the central bank needs to stimulate the economy in order to hit its inflation target. If the economy comes roaring back, the policy rate could be raised, and helicopter money suspended.

Unfortunately, there is no clean way for the central bank to implement such a policy in an independent fashion. The usual way that helicopter money is supposed to work is via the central bank sending "money" to "all" citizens. If the central bank wanted to do this itself, it would need to create a bureaucracy to monitor the eligibility of individuals for the programme. Meanwhile, this programme would likely only dispense payments once or twice per decade. Such a programme would be held up as a classic example of government waste.

Realistically speaking, the programme would need to piggyback on another central government institution that has regular cash transactions with the population. In Canada (and probably most other developed countries), the only infrastructure that meets that definition is the payroll tax withholding system. Tax rates in that system can be tweaked relatively quickly, but doing so does create compliance problems for small businesses if it is done at an irregular time. The reality is that the central bank will not be able to adjust those payroll deduction settings in any more efficient manner than the elected government.

The reliance on an existing distribution framework means that the central bank has no reaction time advantage over the Treasury (which is an alleged advantage of policy rate changes). Furthermore, the slowness of the reaction of fiscal policy is greatly exaggerated. Developed countries reacted very rapidly with fiscal stimulus during the Financial Crisis, including fiscal conservatives, such as the Canadian Conservative Party. Additionally, even if there are implementation lags, expectations matter (to quote our New Keynesian friends). It is very easy to structure tax policies to reward behaviour now, even if the cash reward is delayed (for example, investment/depreciation credits).

We are then stuck with a position that should raise eyebrows: *we cannot trust elected governments to enact discretionary policy because they have a structural tendency to keep fiscal policy too tight.* The only sensible reaction is: no sale.

Developed country central banks were given independence to pursue inflation targeting mandates, as mainstream economists had argued for decades that *politicians had a structural tendency to favour inflationary policies.* Moreover, there is a reason why people listened to that argument: it had a lot of evidence on their side. As the chart above shows, inflation control was not

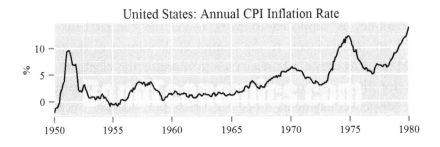

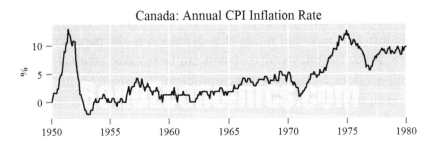

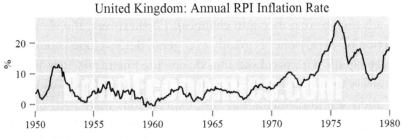

Sources: BLS. Statistics Canada. ONS

Figure 26. *Consumer price inflation in the U.S., Canada, and the U.K.*

exactly a strong point of the post-war "Old Keynesian" policy mix.

Concluding Remarks

It is difficult to see what politico-economic objective helicopter money achieves. Meanwhile, the belief that central banks need fiscal powers because elected officials are structurally averse to deficit spending is a remarkably evidence-free belief.

20 Should We Care About the Origins of Money?

This article is based upon "Should We Care About the History of Money?" (published on May 18, 2016). It has been edited to focus solely on the debate about the origins of money.

When reading about economic theory, one of the arcane areas of argument that comes up is the origin of money. From the perspective that knowledge for the sake of knowledge is a good thing, one cannot complain about this. However, if you are interested in understanding the current monetary system, this debate is largely a red herring.

Barter

Barter is the exchange of goods without the use of money. Although barter should not be of importance in the study of modern industrial economies, it is a topic that unfortunately pops up repeatedly as a result of the structure of economic theories.

A great many classical/neoclassical economics texts (going back to Adam Smith) contained a fairy story along the following lines. During the "Olden Days," people traded goods amongst each other without the use of money. This was inconvenient, as if you had extra shoes but wanted fish, and Bob the Fisherman had fish but only wants pasta, you would need to find a third party who wanted to trade pasta for your shoes. (This is referred to as the "double coincidence of wants" in economics jargon.) A particular good was found to be easier to be in wide demand (such as silver or gold), and then all goods were traded against this common commodity, which became "money" for the society.

The problem with the barter story as it was usually presented was that it was made up, and did not correspond to the facts on the ground. The difficulty is that there are many "non-modern" societies, and each one had its own particularities.

Based on my haphazard survey of the literature, I believe that it would be safe to make the following generalisations.

- "Non-modern" societies organised their economies in a variety of ways, but they generally did not engage in barter amongst themselves (other than some trading that presumably always

takes place amongst individuals). The rules that regulated conduct of members of society also regulated how goods were
distributed.

- When dealing with members of other societies, there was no
  agreed upon moral code that regulated conduct. Trading was
  necessarily of the form of trading goods for goods, or barter.

This complexity means that we cannot say, "barter did not exist," rather
all we can say is that domestic economies were not organised around barter. Furthermore, even if a particular society used a form of money, it
might be forced to use barter transactions with other societies that did not
value the money that it used for internal commerce. That is, money did
not replace the use of barter in the area where it undoubtedly occurred
(inter-group trade).

If the reader is interested in finding more definitive statements regarding barter in "non-modern" societies, I would direct them towards the
anthropological literature. Although this is an interesting area of study, I
doubt that it will help us understand the workings of OECD economies.

The reason that barter comes up in economic discussions is that the
mathematical framework of mainstream economics assumes that barter
transactions are the norm for exchange even in modern societies. Tom
Hickey commented on my original article as follows:[46]

> *The simple answer to the importance of the history of money in theory of
> money is historical. Neoclassical economics is based on the barter-commodity
> theory of money, which implies that money is a neutral veil.*
>
> *The opposition of some economists to this deficient assumption was not only
> to point out that money does not function as a neutral veil in modern monetary
> economics, but also that the narrative on which the barter-commodity theory of
> money is erroneous. For example, the commodity theory leads to the assumption
> that gold is money, or gold, silver and copper are money, and that other forms of
> money are just tokens for these real assets.*
>
> *So, yes, economists have to take the history of money into consideration into
> order to avoid the false assumptions that afflict conventional economic method-*

---

46   "Brian Romanchuk — Should We Care About The History Of
Money?," comment by Tom Hickey on Mike Norman Economics. URL:
http://mikenormaneconomics.blogspot.ca/2016/05/brian-roman-
chuk-should-we-care-about.html

ology, a principal one of which is that a modern economy is a barter economy rather than a monetary economy. This has led to wrong conclusions and disastrous policy based on them.

In my view, whether or not neoclassical economics has false assumptions about money is an empirical question: do the theories generate predictions that fit the facts on the ground? Like most heterodox economists, I would argue that this is indeed the case. The historical origins of these false assumptions are the domain of those interested in the history of thought – which is certainly not my domain of expertise. In any event, this debate does not turn on whether money has its origins in a switch from barter.

Finally, one may note that many free market proponents (such as Austrian economists) argue that barter transactions are the way that society *should* be organised. (Using jargon that economists favour, this is a *normative* statement, not a *positive* statement that just explains observed data.) When the government apparently forces individuals to use state-issued money instead of allowing them to trade in whatever fashion they wish, it is an affront to the economic liberty of those individuals. Although I disagree with that point of view, it is a legitimate position. However, the problem arises when partisans start making up stories about a free market Eden that allegedly used barter, a state from which modern societies have fallen. Using crackpot history to further political beliefs used to be a common tactic, but it now makes no sense in a society with a hyper-developed academic system that churns out far more historical analysis than can possibly be used.

Chartalism

Chartalism could be summarised as "the state theory of money": money is a unit of account that is given value by the taxing power of the state. Probably the only reason that anyone is interested in the theory is that it was adopted by Modern Monetary Theory (MMT).

Chartalism as a school of historical thought was mainly associated with Innes and Knapp, who published about a century ago.

These authors were saved from obscurity as the result of Keynes' approval of Knapp's theory, and his argument that we have had "state money" for 4000 years. (Hence, the usage "modern money" in "Modern Monetary Theory" was a bit of an in-joke.) The MMT version of Chartalism is focussed more on how taxes drive the value of the money, rather than its historical origins, and is sometimes called "neo-Chartalism" to distinguish it from the earlier version of the theory. For further reading, I would recommend:

- "The Hierarchy of Money," by Stephanie Bell (Kelton).[47]
- *Understanding Modern Money*, L. Randall Wray.[48]

In contrast to the Chartalists, the "Metallists" argued that money has its roots in barter, and that it started as a metal that was valued based upon its weight. Stephanie Bell (Kelton) summarised the Metallist view (in the paper cited above) as:

> *Money is said to arise spontaneously in the private sector in order to eliminate some of the inefficiencies of barter. Thus, society agrees upon some means of exchange called "money" in order to overcome some of the transaction costs associated with barter.*
>
> *The Metallists maintained that society settled on a metallic currency (gold, silver, etc.) so that the money would have (intrinsic) value.*

The argument between the historical Chartalists and Metallists revolved around whether "the state" was involved in the creation and regulation of money in various historical societies. The modern Chartalists ("neo-Chartalists") have continued this debate, although the analysis is based on more modern historical scholarship.

Anwar Shaikh, who is critical of neo-Chartalism, notes in his book *Capitalism: Competition, Conflict, Crises*[49]:

> *This whole unpersuasive and inconclusive line of argument* [discussing Randall Wray's discussion of monetary history- BR] *is puzzling until one recalls that he is trying to extend back some 4,000 years the particular claim that the modern fiat-money-issuing state determines the price level because it sets*

47   "The Hierarchy of Money," Stephanie Bell (Kelton), Jerome Levy Economics Institute, Working Paper No. 231, April 1998. URL: http://www.levyinstitute.org/pubs/wp/231.pdf

48   *Understanding Modern Money: The Key to Full Employment and Price Stability,* by L. Randall Wray, Edward Elgar, 1998. ISBN: 978 1 84542 941 6.

49   Quotation found in the section "Modern Chartalism," in Chapter 15 of *Capitalism: Competition, Conflict, Crises,* by Anwar Shaikh. Published in 2016 by the Oxford University Press, eBook ISBN: 9780190298340.

the money wage via the ELR [Employer of Last Resort, or Job Guarantee programme – BR].

Although Anwar Shaikh's criticisms of neo-Chartalist history are comprehensive, I found some aspects of them somewhat unpersuasive. If the reader is interested in the topic, I would highly suggest reading *Capitalism.* That said, I view most of the argument about the origins of money to be an eccentric academic debate, and of secondary importance. (As an eccentric ex-academic myself, I understand that such debates are entertaining for many people, but are not of wider significance.)

As the Shaikh quotation highlights, what matters is the application to modern societies. Historical examples can be used to illustrate points, but the exact nature of Babylonian commerce does not really affect how we should organise contemporary societies.

In the present day, there are echoes of these debates. The key question is: why does a fiat currency have any value? (Alternatively, what determines the price level, which can be viewed as the inverse of the value of money.) I offer three simplified explanations (which reflect different schools of thought).

1. Fiat money derives its value from the demand created by taxes, or in other words, "taxes drive money." *(This is the neo-Chartalist view.)*

2. Fiat money is just a bubble, and it will eventually disappear in a puff of hyperinflation. Societies will return to the use of precious metal-backed currency. *(This is a typical view of gold standard supporters.)*

3. Money has some mystical powers in commerce, which causes people to value it. Alternatively, the central bank will destroy the economy (somehow) if people refuse to keep the price level where the central bank wants it to be. *(Variations of these ideas show up in mainstream/Monetarist views.)*

When we structure the debate in this fashion, we can then attempt to make predictions about modern economies. I am obviously biased towards the neo-Chartalist viewpoint, but one should note that it is possible to find any number of examples that could prove almost anything (such as privately issued tokens that retain value despite having no tax backing, etc.). However, I would note that macroeconomics is almost entirely concerned with state-issued fiat currency, and none of the major industrial democracies would even dream about removing the tax backing from their currencies.[50]

This debate would survive even if we abolish "money" from economic theory. We would still need government liabilities within models; for example, we could have models where the only government-issued liabilities are one-period Treasury bills. The notional value of the Treasury bills acts as a unit of account, allowing us to define a price level. We can still ask ourselves what determines the price level within this simplified economy (or why are model entities willing to trade real goods and services for Treasury bills)?

Concluding Remarks

History is a legitimate area of academic enquiry, and the history of money is interesting to many (based on the evidence of the number of books written on the subject). However, if you ever find yourself sucked into a debate about the monetary practices of some society, I would recommend comparing the dates involved versus a current calendar, and asking yourself whether the topic under dispute really matters.

---

50   As always, we can come up with exceptions. For example, we could imagine a country with ample natural resources and a state-controlled extraction agency abolishing domestic taxation (think of petro-states). The natural resources would effectively back the state-issued currency. I would view this as a natural extension of neo-Chartalism; foreign consumers of the exported natural resources are the ones paying the "tax" that is backing the currency. A linguistic purist might disagree with that usage of the word tax, but as usual, I do not really care about such bickering over wording.

21 Abolishing Currency in the Real World Is Just Plain Nuts

This article is a rewritten version of "Negative Interest Rates and Abolishing Cash," published on January 3, 2015.

Although I like the choice of title for this book, it would be easy to mistake it as being part of the literature that calls for abolition of currency in the real world. As the title of this essay suggests, I have some doubts about such a policy move.

Why Abolish Currency?

Under normal circumstances, proposals to change the monetary system come from crackpots or ideologues. However, in the case of abolishing currency, the proponents tend to be mainstream economists, quite often with strong academic pedigree.

The logic behind abolishing currency is straightforward. Instead of being able to use notes and coins in transactions, all monetary transfers would be electronic. Once we move to having all "money" as being the equivalent of a bank balance, there is very little stopping the central bank from setting the policy rate as negative.

The *belief* amongst (most) mainstream economists is that once the nominal rate of interest is sufficiently below the rate of inflation, economic activity will take off. (Admittedly, there are some debates within the mainstream about that statement, but they occur at the fringe.) The dreaded zero bound is what has trapped the developed economies in "secular stagnation." *(At the time of writing, Donald Trump has just won the election, but has not taken office. Fears about "secular stagnation" may be replaced by screaming about "fiscal sustainability" in short order.)*

The Problems With Electronic Money

The problems with electronic money are relatively straightforward.
- Destruction of anonymity. Every single transaction you make will become part of your permanent record.
- Trust. Do I want to provide access to my electronic payment

credentials to everyone I need to deal with monetarily? Do I hand my children my debit card so that they can go buy some milk from the store?

- Barrier to entry. Are small children going to have to set up a merchant account so that they can run a lemonade stand?
- Techno-optimism. We are moving to a world based on intermittent sources of electrical power; putting into place a scheme that relies on a perfectly functioning grid is dangerous.
- Resource wastage. Considerable efforts will be expended to find ways to avoid being hit by negative interest rates. The resources expended on such schemes are a loss to society.

The Indian Demonetisation Debacle

There has been one real-world experiment in "demonetisation" which was kicked off in November 2016[51]. It should be noted that despite being called "demonetisation," it did not attempt to eliminate currency. Instead, 500 and 1000 rupee notes were pulled from circulation, to be replaced by 2000 rupee notes. The notes being replaced represented 86% of the currency in circulation. The objective was to force people to return their cash hoards to banks, so that they would become visible to the tax authorities.

However, these 2000 rupee notes were too large a denomination to be useful for day-to-day purposes, and India still has a very large cash-based economy. It has been argued that the authorities chose to issue a higher denomination note because of the inability to print the higher volumes of notes that might be useful for commerce in the short run.

I will not pretend to have any expertise on the Indian economy, nor do I have strong confidence in my assessment of the true effects of the policy. That said, the reportage I have seen from India suggests that this policy has been an utter fiasco, which has resulted in unnecessary deaths.

From the point of view of economic theory, this episode is interesting. As was pointed out by Ramanan, a policy that eliminates almost the entire stock of currency does raise the issue that the Monetarists were correct in arguing that money is needed for commerce.[52]

---

51   Thanks to reader Jerry Brown for spotting that I had the wrong date in the ebook edition.

52   The article by Ramanan appeared as "Remonetisation," on

My view is that this episode just proves that bad policies lead to bad outcomes. Any policy that blows up the payments system is going to have a negative effect on commercial activity; whether that has anything to do with *"M"* in an economic model is an open question. Meanwhile, this event could be viewed as a form of selective default: certain instruments issued by the government had their usefulness and value revoked because of a policy change. If a government defaulted on its debts, it would similarly cause chaos within the payments system, and would wipe out the liquidity position of many within the private sector (causing cascading defaults). As a result, the problems caused by demonetisation are not exclusive to money versus government liabilities more generally.

In any event, the episode underlines that the authorities do not have the ability to set the level of the "money supply," which was a key tenet of Monetarism.

It is unclear how much we could generalise this experience to the hypothetical case of another government attempting a more gradual movement towards electronic money, but it does demonstrate that things can go rapidly wrong when technocrats attempt social engineering by messing around with money.

Negative Rates Will Not Work In the First Place

The other problem with the idea of abolishing cash to allow negative interest rates is that it is entirely faith-based. As I discussed in *Interest Rate Cycles: An Introduction*, the belief that negative interest rates will stimulate economic growth is entirely based on models where this outcome is *assumed* to happen. Furthermore, the empirical methods used to validate mainstream economic models also embed the same assumption, and so they could not reject the possibility that the assumption is wrong.

We saw this behaviour in real time after the Financial Crisis. The consensus was that interest rates were "unsustainably low" in 2010, and that the U.S. economy would take off like a rocket thereafter. Once said lift-off failed to occur, lo and behold, the empirical models revised down the estimated natural rate of interest, so that the nominal rates had to be negative in order to stimulate the economy.

the website Concerted Action. URL: http://www.concertedaction. com/2016/11/14/remonetisation/

We should not pay a lot of attention to circular logic like this. We need to go back to first principles, and try to figure out what is going on.

A negative interest rate is a form of a tax on the monetary base. *Making the policy rate more negative would increase that tax.* It is difficult to see why we should *assume* that such a move is going to increase economic growth.

Concluding Remarks

One can only hope that a burst of inflationary growth will kill off this idea. Unfortunately, the policy consensus that gave the developed world synchronised low inflation stagnation is going to be difficult to break. It would likely arise in the next global downturn if nominal interest rates have not made a decent dash from 0%.

Part IV: Looking Forward

22 Financial Assets Matter, Not Money

This article has not been previously published.

If we abolish money from economic theory, what replaces it? The answer is: financial assets. Although this might be viewed as a superficial change, there are important implications. In particular, the central bank can manipulate the amount outstanding of some types of financial assets, but it cannot control all of them. We end up with a more realistic view of central bank power. They no longer control "money" and hence all commerce, rather they are reduced to worrying about setting interest rates.

The Role of Financial Assets in Economic Models

A properly defined macroeconomic model consists of three things:
1. the sectors of the economy that define the model,
2. the accounting relationships amongst those sectors, and
3. the behavioural rules the sectors follow.

There is no doubt that the behavioural rules are important, as they define the operating characteristics of a model. However, we also need to make sure we properly track the accounting relationships between the sectors.

One somewhat silly example I used on my website illustrates the importance of accounting. I took a standard extremely simple stock-flow consistent (SFC) model, and then modified the behaviour of the business sector. (Stock-flow consistent models are a standard form of models used by post-Keynesians.)

In the standard version of the model, the business sector had a 0% profit margin; it hired enough workers so that the wage bill equalled the business sector revenue. I modified this behaviour to the following: the business sector always ensured that it had a 10% profit margin.

Although it sounds like an innocuous change, the model behaviour was greatly modified. Since I had not specified what the business sector was doing with its profits, it ended up accumulating an increasing stock of financial assets. In turn, this forced the government to run perpetual deficits, as it was the sole supplier of financial assets. (In the base case model, the government moved towards a balanced budget, as the stock of financial assets converged to a fixed amount.)

The model was unrealistic, but it illustrated a key point: we need to look at the entire macroeconomic system, and the linkages between sectors, in order to predict the effect of behavioural changes. There is a widespread belief that the government determines the level of the fiscal deficit. However, In this case, the perpetual deficits were the result of a change in business sector behaviour.

Financial Assets as the Glue in Models

Mainstream economic theorists want to focus on real variables: the number of widgets produced, the number of people working, etc. Financial assets are just supposed to be a "veil" over the underlying real transactions. This belief is an underlying reason why mainstream models are uniformly terrible in describing the real world.

More realistic models account for the fact that the world is uncertain; we do not know exactly how much we will earn or spend over the coming year. When outcomes deviate from plans, we need to use financial assets to buffer the uncertainty. For example, if we spend more than we expected during the month, we either have to run down our financial assets (or borrow, which is issuing a financial asset to the lender).

Within a model, the change in financial assets for a sector is equal to the sum of all of the transactions that sector has with the other sectors. Meanwhile, the breakdown of which financial assets are held depends on the model's assumptions for portfolio weighting behaviour. For example, the household sector might allocate between zero-interest cash and interest-bearing bonds and bills based on the (real) interest rate.

Historically, economists said that *money* acted as the buffer stock for uncertainty. However, that is not true, other than for very short time horizons (which we cannot hope to model). Households, firms, and governments do not just adjust their money holdings in response to surprises; they adjust their entire balance sheet of financial assets and liabilities. Although the instruments in the various measures of the money supply are convenient for settlement, the big movements in balance sheets may be in long-term financial assets.

The following essay, "Money in SFC Models," gives a more detailed analysis.

Concluding Remarks

Replacing "money" with "financial assets" may appear innocuous, but it delivers us from the delusion that central banks have arbitrary power to steer the economy.

23 Money in SFC Models

This is an expanded version of "Primer: Money and Debt in SFC Models," which appeared on April 10, 2016.

How money and debt are described in simple economic models colours economists' interpretation of real-world monetary systems. My feeling is that money is somewhat superfluous in these models, but it is necessary to understand why that is the case. This article explains how money and government debt (Treasury bills) operate in the second simplest Stock-Flow Consistent (SFC) model in the textbook *Monetary Economics* by Godley and Lavoie[53] – model PC (Portfolio Choice; found in Chapter 4).

If the reader is familiar with mainstream models – like Dynamic Stochastic General Equilibrium models (DSGE) – the treatment of money and debt is generally similar to model PC. There are a number of convention differences, which means that the formulae look different, but they quite often imply the same behaviour. The real differences show up in the philosophy of the solution of the model, which actually should not affect how money and debt operate as instruments. In the interests of brevity, I will defer the discussion of these differences to later. However, understanding how money and debt work within an SFC model – which can be cleanly solved – will prepare readers to understand the less well-defined DSGE models.

Description of Model PC

Model PC is found in Chapter 4 of *Monetary Economics: An Integrated Approach to Credit, Money, Income, Production and Wealth*, by Wynne Godley and Marc Lavoie.

For those of you without the text, the models are available online at the *sfc-models* website: http://models.sfc-models.net/. The number of equations is impressive for what is actually a fairly simple model.

Model PC builds upon Model SIM (which refers to the simplest SFC model). Figure 27 on page 152 depicts the cash flows. Model SIM only has

53   *Monetary Economics: An Integrated Approach to Credit, Money, Income, Production and Wealth (Second Edition)*, Wynne Godley and Marc Lavoie, Palgrave Macmillan, 2012. ISBN: 978-0-230-30184-9.

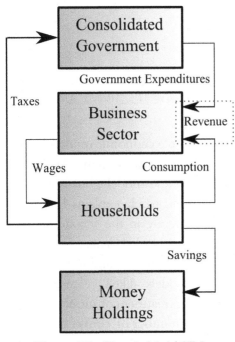

Figure 27. *Flows in Model SIM.*

"money" – which bears no interest – as a financial asset. It is denoted H within the equations, as it is what is referred to in economist jargon as "high-powered money."

Note that Government Expenditures (denoted G) is an exogenous variable that drives the system. All other variables are determined by it and the stock of government money held at the end of the previous period. The government generally uses deficit financing, issuing money (which it creates at no real cost) in consequence. If money were gold-backed, we would need to track the government's gold holdings within the model, as that would limit the ability to issue money.

I have labelled the government as "Consolidated Government." This entity includes the Treasury (fiscal agency) and the central bank.

Within the model, the business sector has the apparently magical ability to hire exactly enough workers so that total revenues equal its wage bill. Since the business sector is always just breaking even, it pays no tax. This is unrealistic (perhaps other than the taxation part), but relaxing this assumption greatly increases the model complexity – otherwise, we need to allow the business sector to have a mismatched production and sales. That possibility would imply the need to track inventory, and business sector holdings of money. The number of state variables within the model would rapidly increase. Although we can solve those more complex models numerically, intuition is harder to come by.

(It should be noted that later models introduce expectation errors by households and businesses, at the cost of added complexity. The magical forecasting ability of the business sector within models SIM and PC is not a general property of SFC models.)

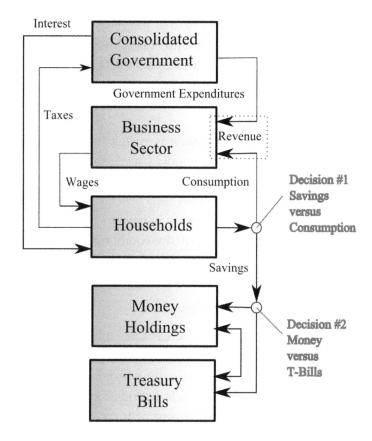

Figure 28. *Flows in Model PC.*

With the business sector behaviour locked down, the diagram makes it clear that there is only one decision to be made within the model – how will the household sector allocate its income between consumption and saving? Once that decision is reached, all other behaviour is determined by the income flows. The decision itself is reached via a consumption function.

Figure 28 illustrates the flows within Model PC. There are three functional differences from model SIM.

1. The government pays interest upon Treasury bills (which are only held by households outside the consolidated government).

2. The household sector now faces two decisions, which are highlighted on the diagram. It first needs to decide how much to consume out of its income (wages plus interest), and it then needs to decide upon its portfolio allocation between money

and Treasury bills. (Note that the allocation decision covers the entire portfolio, and not just cash inflows for the period.)

3. The interest rate on Treasury bills acts as a new external (exogenous) variable.

New Financial Assets

Within the SFC model framework, it is straightforward to add new asset classes, at the cost of increasing model complexity. The decision process is similar – the household first decides the level of consumption, and then the asset weightings in the portfolio.

The issue with adding new assets is how to model their prices. Is it possible to reflect the behaviour of the equity market within a simplified model? The risk is that small behavioural differences can result in completely different outcomes.

Government Budget Constraint

Within the mainstream literature, there is a fair amount of mysticism about the "governmental budget constraint." With SFC models, the dubious "inter-temporal" component disappears (the condition on infinite time horizons), and all that matters is the single-period accounting constraint.

All this constraint says is that government accounting properly follows the rules of double-entry accounting. This is not particularly interesting, other than by comparison to some older mainstream models where the accounting was not done correctly.

Consolidation and the Portfolio Allocation Decision

Within model PC, the household decisions are hierarchical. The household sector first decides on the level of consumption for the period. (This is based on starting wealth, interest, and wage income.) The remainder is saved, which increases the value of its portfolio of financial assets (money and Treasury bills).

The portfolio is allocated between money and Treasury bills. Since money does not pay interest, it is less attractive as interest rates climb. Hence, the allocation function depends upon the level of interest rates.

This raises an obvious issue – how can the household sector change its portfolio allocation? The business sector holds no financial assets, and there are no other non-government sectors. (The foreign

sector has not yet been introduced.) Therefore, by process of elimi-
nation, the portfolio allocation decision by households must be ac-
commodated by the consolidated government sector. That is, the
consolidated government must adjust the money and Treasury bill
outstanding amounts to match the whims of the household sector.

The mechanism that allows this is the central bank. It holds Treasury
bills as assets, and issues money as a liability. Since money pays no interest,
and there is no possibility of capital gains/losses on Treasury bills within
the model, the central bank earns a steady profit from interest payments on
its portfolio. The central bank is then assumed to pay the profits immediately back to the Treasury, so that the total interest cost for the government
is just the interest paid on Treasury bills owned by the non-government.

Determination of Interest Rates and the Monetary Base

Within the SFC model, the level of interest rates is fixed by the central bank (and is external to the model). The amount of money held is
entirely determined by the portfolio preference of households. This
corresponds to "normal" central bank behaviour, where the policy
committee sets the level of interest rates, and the money supply is determined by private sector behaviour; the central bank has to engage in open market operations to keep the overnight rate near target.

Alternatively, if the portfolio allocation function is obliging, the central
bank could target the amount of money in the system. The central bank
adjusts the interest rate until the money supply hits target. Within the context of this model, there is no way of distinguishing the targeting regime.
This ambiguity also appears in mainstream models, which allows silliness
like exogenous money to take root.

In the real world, the size of the money supply is driven by more
complicated factors. For example, in the United States, banks need
to hold reserves against certain types of deposits. The interchange-
ability of interest rates and the money supply starts to break down.

If the interest rate is zero, there is nothing that distinguishes a Treasury bill from money within the model. In such a case, the central bank
can push the allocation back and forth how it wants. However, these allocation changes make no observable differences to model outcomes
from the perspective of the private sector. (In the real world, there

might be minor institutional differences between the instruments.)

As a result, the notion of Quantitative Easing (QE) makes little sense within model PC. The only assets the central bank can purchase are Treasury bills. The only way the central bank can increase the monetary base is via lowering interest rates, until it hits 0%. At which point, it is free to push the money/bills allocation around, but that has no effect on households – it has exactly the same interest income regardless of allocation, which is zero.

Concluding Remarks

To what extent money appears in a SFC model, it is just another financial asset, and its level is determined by a portfolio allocation decision within the private sector. There is no reason to believe that its level can drive economic activity in any particular direction.

End Matter

Data Sources

This text relies upon data that has come from a variety of national sources. In some cases, the data are calculated by one agency, but distributed by another. My charts list the data sources used (in abbreviated form).

- **Canada.** Canadian data used was either calculated by Statistics Canada or the Bank of Canada. All data have been downloaded from the CANSIM delivery platform. URL: http://www5.statcan. gc.ca/cansim/home-accueil?lang=eng&p2=50&HPA

- **United States.** The United States has a number of agencies that generate statistical data. I most commonly use the Bureau of Economic Analysis (BEA) as well as the Bureau of Labor Statistics (BLS). For most of these sources, I download the data from the Federal Reserve Economic Data (FRED) website, which is a service provided by the St. Louis Federal Reserve Bank. (Other sources for U.S. data are noted below.) URL: http://research.stlouisfed. org/fred2/

- **United States Flow of Funds.** This is the Z.1 release, which is calculated by the Board of Governors of the Federal Reserve System. It is a comprehensive database of stocks and flows of financial assets. Given the number of series involved, it is easier to download the entire block of Z.1 data than on a series-by-series basis from FRED. URL: http://www.federalreserve.gov/releases/ z1/

- **IMF.** The IMF publishes World Economic Outlook (WEO) database, which contains historical data as well as forecasts. One of the advantages of these data is that they are presented using a consistent set of national accounting concepts. URL: https://www.imf. org/external/ns/cs.aspx?id=28

- **Office of National Statistics (ONS) – United Kingdom.** The ONS is a centralised source for data for the United Kingdom. URL: https://www.ons.gov.uk/

Calculations and plotting are done in the R computer language. Plots are generated using the *ggplot2* package.)

Also by BondEconomics

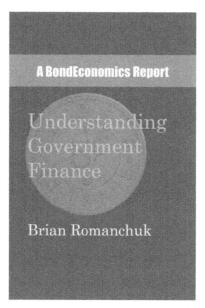

Understanding Government Finance (June 2015)

The government budget is not like a household budget. This report introduces the financial operations used by a central government with a free-floating currency, and explains how they differ from that of a household or corporation. The focus is on the types of constraints such a government faces.

This report introduces a simplified framework for the monetary system, along with the operating procedures that are associated with it. Some of the complications seen in real-world government finance are then added onto this simplified framework.

This report also acts as an introduction to some of the concepts used by Modern Monetary Theory, a school of thought within economics. Modern Monetary Theory emphasises the real limits of government action, as opposed to purely theoretical views about fiscal policy.

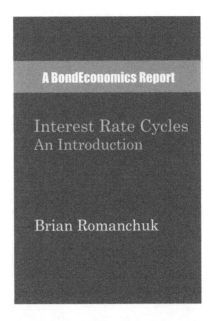

Interest Rate Cycles: An Introduction (June 2016)

Monetary policy has increasingly become the focus of economists and investors. This report describes the factors driving interest rates across the economic cycle. Written by an experienced fixed income analyst, it explains in straightforward terms the theory that lies behind central bank thinking. Although monetary theory appears complex and highly mathematical, the text explains how decisions still end up being based upon qualitative views about the state of the economy. The text makes heavy use of charts of historical data to illustrate economic concepts and modern monetary history. The report is informal, but contains references and suggestions for further reading.

About the Author

Brian Romanchuk founded BondEconomics.com in 2013. It is a website dedicated to providing analytical tools for the understanding of the bond markets and monetary economics.

He previously was a senior fixed income analyst at *la Caisse de dépôt et placement du Québec*. He held a few positions, including being the head of quantitative analysis for fixed income. He worked there from 2006-2013. Previously, he worked as a quantitative analyst at BCA Research, a Montréal-based economic-financial research consultancy, from 1998-2005. During that period, he developed a number of proprietary models for fixed income analysis, as well as covering the economies of a few developed countries.

Brian received a Ph.D. in Control Systems Engineering from the University of Cambridge, and held post-doctoral positions there and at McGill University. His undergraduate degree was in electrical engineering, from McGill. He is a CFA charter holder.

Brian currently lives in the greater Montréal area.

Index

Lightning Source UK Ltd.
Milton Keynes UK
UKOW06f1902270417
300068UK00007B/478/P